# Single-Session Therapy

G000244378

*Single-Session Therapy: Distinctive Features* provides a general introduction to the field of Single-Session Therapy (SST). Written by eminent clinician and author Windy Dryden, this book challenges mainstream therapeutic assumptions, predicated on the certainty that clients will have more than one therapy session. This book follows the popular Distinctive Features format and is divided into two sections, describing 15 theoretical features and 15 practical techniques of SST.

*Single-Session Therapy* will be of interest to those across the psychotherapy and counselling professions and will provide extensive guidance for students and practitioners alike.

**Windy Dryden** is in clinical and consultative practice and is an international authority on Cognitive Behaviour Therapy. He is Emeritus Professor of Psychotherapeutic Studies at Goldsmiths, University of London. He has worked in psychotherapy for more than 40 years and is the author of over 225 books.

# Psychotherapy and Counselling Distinctive Features

Series Editor: Windy Dryden

The Psychotherapy and Counselling Distinctive Features series provides readers with an introduction to the distinctive theoretical and practical features of various therapeutic approaches from leading practitioners in their field.

Each book in this series focuses on one particular approach and guides the reader through 30 features – both theoretical and practical – that are particularly distinctive of that approach. Written for practitioners by practitioners, this series will also be of interest to trainees, social workers and many others outside the therapeutic tradition.

**Titles in the series:**

*Pluralistic Therapy* by John McLeod

*Cognitive Analytic Therapy* by Claire Corbridge, Laura Brummer and Philippa Coid

*Existential Therapy* by Emmy van Deurzen and Claire Arnold-Baker

*Strengths-Based Therapy* by John J. Murphy and Jacqueline A. Sparks

*Single-Session Therapy* by Windy Dryden

For further information about this series please visit:

www.routledge.com/Psychotherapy-and-Counselling-Distinctive-Features/
book-series/PCDF

# Single-Session Therapy

## Distinctive Features

## Windy Dryden

Routledge
Taylor & Francis Group

LONDON AND NEW YORK

First published 2019
by Routledge
2 Park Square, Milton Park, Abingdon, Oxon OX14 4RN

and by Routledge
52 Vanderbilt Avenue, New York, NY 10017

*Routledge is an imprint of the Taylor & Francis Group, an informa business*

*British Library Cataloguing-in-Publication Data*
A catalogue record for this book is available from the British Library

*Library of Congress Cataloging-in-Publication Data*
Names: Dryden, Windy, author.
Title: Single-session therapy : distinctive features / Windy Dryden.
Description: Milton Park, Abingdon, Oxon ; New York, NY : Routledge, 2019. |
Series: Psychotherapy and counselling distinctive features |
Includes bibliographical references and index.
Identifiers: LCCN 2018047077 (print) | LCCN 2018048084 (ebook) |
ISBN 9780429024313 (Master) | ISBN 9780429656613 (ePub) |
ISBN 9780429659058 (Web PDF) | ISBN 9780429654176 (Mobi/Kindle) |
ISBN 9780367110130 (hardback: alk. paper) |
ISBN 9780367110116 (pbk. : alk. paper) | ISBN 9780429024313 (ebk)
Subjects: LCSH: Single-session psychotherapy.
Classification: LCC RC480.55 (ebook) |
LCC RC480.55 .D77 2019 (print) | DDC 616.89/14–dc23
LC record available at https://lccn.loc.gov/2018047077

ISBN: 978-0-367-11013-0 (hbk)
ISBN: 978-0-367-11011-6 (pbk)
ISBN: 978-0-429-02431-3 (ebk)

Typeset in Times New Roman
by Newgen Publishing UK

Printed and bound in Great Britain by
TJ International Ltd, Padstow, Cornwall

# Contents

Preface                                                                vii
Acknowledgements                                                        xi

**Part 1  THEORY**                                                       **1**
 1  What's in a name                                                  3
 2  Misconceptions about SST                                          7
 3  People have the capacity to help themselves quickly             11
 4  SST is based on providing help at the point of need
   rather than help at the point of availability           15
 5  The SST mindset                                                  21
 6  The importance of expectations in SST                           26
 7  SST is a fusion between what the client brings to the
   process and what the therapist brings to the process   30
 8  SST challenges therapists' cherished beliefs about
   therapy and change                                       35
 9  What can be achieved from SST                                    39
10  The 'client criteria' question                                      44
11  What makes good SST therapists                                      51
12  For better or for worse: Context matters                            56
13  The importance of the working alliance                              59
14  From theory to practice I: Guidelines for good practice             65
15  From theory to practice II: What to avoid                           72

**Part 2 PRACTICE** **79**

16  Overview: The process of SST                              81
17  Making a decision about SST                               86
18  Preparing for the session                                 90
19  Contracting                                               95
20  Getting started                                           99
21  Working with problems and goals                          105
22  Creating and maintaining a session focus                 110
23  Doing the work                                           114
24  Utilising client variables                               121
25  Making an impact                                         126
26  Negotiating a solution                                   131
27  Practising the solution in the session                   135
28  Bringing the session to a suitable end                   140
29  Encouraging client reflection, digestion,
    action and decision                                      144
30  Following-through and following-up                       148

References                                                   152
Index                                                        158

# Preface

Single-Session Therapy (SST) is not new. Sigmund Freud, the father of psychoanalysis (hardly a brief therapy), was reported to have carried out two well-known single-session treatments with Aurelia Öhm-Kronich ('Katharina') in 1893 (Freud & Breuer, 1895) and with the famous composer, Gustav Mahler, in 1910 (Kuehn, 1965). Alfred Adler, who split from Freud to develop what eventually became known as Adlerian Therapy, established a number of child guidance clinics in the 1920s where he would do single-session demonstrations of his technique with parents and children, separately and together, in front of a mixed professional and lay audience. For 40 years (from 1965 to 2005), Albert Ellis did single-session therapy with volunteer members of a largely lay audience at the Institute that bore his name (Ellis & Joffe, 2002). Most of Milton Erickson's known cases lasted for a single session (O'Hanlon & Hexum, 1990) and the famous 'Gloria' films where 'Gloria' was interviewed by Carl Rogers, Fritz Perls and Albert Ellis in 1965 can be seen as single-session therapies.

To some degree, SST lost its way in the 1970s and early 1980s despite important work by Bernard Bloom (1981). It was not until the early 1990s when Moshe Talmon (1990) published his seminal book entitled *Single-Session Therapy: Maximising the Effect of the First (and Often Only) Therapeutic Encounter*, reporting on work carried out at the Kaiser Permanente Clinic in California with his colleagues Michael Hoyt and Robert Rosenbaum, that interest was rekindled in SST.

Since then and increasingly since 2012 when the first international conference on SST and walk-in therapy was held in Melbourne, Australia followed by the second international conference in Banff, Canada in 2015,[1] SST has attracted much attention as the world grapples to offer therapeutic help at the point of need rather than at the point of availability.

Training in psychotherapy and counselling is still predicated on the idea that clients will certainly have more than one session. This is the case even though worldwide, the most frequent number of sessions people have is 'one' (Hoyt & Talmon, 2014a; Hoyt, Bobele, Slive, Young & Talmon, 2018a). This 'wake-up' call provides the backdrop for this book.

As with other books in the 'Psychotherapy and Counselling Distinctive Features' series, this volume is divided into two parts: theory and practice with 15 distinctive features discussed in each part. Unlike other books in the series, *Single-Session Therapy* is not an approach. Rather, as you will see, it is a mindset which underpins a way of working that practitioners from diverse approaches can adopt. The SST community is a broad church with therapists working with individuals, couples and groups (Hoyt & Talmon, 2014b, Hoyt, Bobele, Slive, Young & Talmon, 2018b). My own SST practice is with individuals and although I have tried to write a book that people from the SST community would think is fair-minded, I do have my biases. When I have drawn upon my own experience, I have tried to make this clear. Having said that, this book is far more general scope than a book I wrote for my 'CBT Distinctive Features' series (Dryden, 2017) entitled *Single-Session Integrated Cognitive Behaviour Therapy (SSI-CBT): Distinctive Features*.

Please be aware that this book is likely to challenge mainstream therapeutic beliefs. I hope that you will read it with an open mind. If you do, it might change your practice for the better.

## *Note*

1   A third international conference is planned, again near Melbourne, Australia, for late 2019.

# Acknowledgements

I wish to thank 'Reach Out Centre for Kids, Ontario, Canada' for permission to reproduce questions from their Walk-in Counselling Clinic Client Questionnaire (2017) – see Table 18.1.

# THEORY

THEORY

# What's in a name

## Abstract

*In this opening chapter, I consider the nature of single-session therapy (SST) by discussing some of the ways in which it has been defined. This shows that while on the surface it is clear what SST is – it is a therapy that lasts for one session – actually the situation is more complex than that.*

## SST is one session only

As I have just said, the term 'Single-Session Therapy' (SST) seems clear. It means one session of therapy, and that is it. While some people in the field may see it this way, most contemporary SST therapists disagree with this view as we shall presently see.

## Talmon's (1990) definition

One of the pioneers of SST, Moshe Talmon (1990) provided a different definition in his seminal book. He said, "Single-session therapy is defined here as one face-to-face meeting between a therapist and a patient with no previous or subsequent sessions within one year" (Talmon, 1990: xv). This means that the therapist and client could have non-face-to-face meetings and the therapy could still be regarded as SST.

## Hoyt et al.'s (2018a) refinement

Recently, Hoyt, Bobele, Slive, Young & Talmon (2018a) distanced themselves from Talmon's (1990) definition, which they say was used for research purposes. They argue that the point that there should be no other sessions in the year before or after was arbitrary and the 'face-to-face' criterion predated the development of online communication platforms such as Skype. They make the point that the work discussed in Talmon's book was based on the fact that many people attend only one session, and consequently, therapist and client are advised to approach the first session *as if* it were going to be the last. Twenty-eight years after the publication of Talmon's book, Hoyt et al. (2018a: 18, footnote) say the following: "SST clients may be seen more than once in a year (nowadays either face-to-face or via telephone or online), and the basic SST desideratum is that a session be approached as though it could be the only (single) session, complete unto itself". However, as most SST theorists and therapists now stress, if a client needs further sessions they should be made available to the person. This more nuanced view where the session is treated as if it were to be the only session, but that further sessions are available if requested by the client, is perhaps the most dominant in the field of SST today.

## One-at-a-Time (OAAT) Therapy

Michael Hoyt (2011) introduced the term 'One-At-A-Time Therapy' to the literature. This term has been accepted by the SST community as shown by its inclusion in the title of Hoyt et al.'s (2018b) book. However, as we shall see, it lacks the impact of the term 'single-session therapy'. As the term suggests, 'One-at-a-Time' Therapy is a therapy that occurs one session at a time. The client is informed that one session of therapy may suffice, but if not, they can book another session. What they cannot do is to book a series of sessions. My view is that in OAAT Therapy, the therapist can encourage the client to reflect on the session that they have had, digest what they have learned, put such learning into practice, and then let things settle before deciding whether or not to book another session (see Chapter 29).

OAAT Therapy fits with what Nicholas Cummings (1990) called brief intermittent psychotherapy through the life cycle. Here, a person would seek therapy when they had a problem which they could not solve by themself. They would leave therapy when they felt able to address the problem independently. The OAAT framework allows the person to address their problem one session at a time, to come and go, as it were, and return whenever they feel that they could benefit from therapy.

Michael Hoyt (2018, 4th May, personal communication), who came up with the term 'OAAT' Therapy, said:

> Sometimes I say 'One-at-a-time doesn't necessarily mean only one time'. Young (2018) makes the point that SST is really a misnomer (since many people return) but argues that we should retain the term 'SST' because it is 'in your face' and disruptively challenges the notion that therapy must be multi-sessioned or continuous.

This adds an additional dimension to the name debate. While the term 'One-at-a-Time' Therapy may be more accurate, it has less impact than SST. SST has also been in use for far longer, although the term has its problems. Albert Ellis, the founder of Rational Emotive Behaviour Therapy (REBT), used to make a similar point about the word 'rational'. In his workshops, Ellis would say that if he had his time over again and with the benefit of hindsight he would have called his therapy 'Cognitive Emotive Behaviour Therapy'. However, the word 'rational' was in such frequent use when referring to REBT that to change it at such a late stage would be counterproductive.

## SST by design and SST by default

It is important to distinguish between SST by design and SST by default. SST by design occurs when the therapist and client intentionally embark on single-session therapy. This could be a single session with no prospect of further sessions or one where one or more sessions are possible. The critical point is that both the therapist and client agree on this before embarking on therapy.

SST by default occurs when a client attends one session when both therapist and client anticipate that therapy would involve a longer-term contract. Here, the client has decided not to attend another session. In this case, they may cancel the next scheduled appointment or not turn up for it. Therapists often refer to clients who do not return for a second session as 'drop-outs' from treatment, mainly if a client does not show up for an appointment that they have not cancelled. In short, SST by default tends to be seen as therapy dropout, and this is generally viewed negatively by therapists who think that the client has derived little or no benefit from the session that they had. Actually, and surprisingly perhaps, when SST is by default most clients are satisfied with the session that they have had and consider that they have received the help that they were looking for (Hoyt et al., 2018a; Talmon, 1990).

While OAAT Therapy is usually by design, it may be that the therapy evolved into this way of working as the person leaves when they have been helped and return when they need more help.

## SST by appointment or walk-in

Finally, SST may occur by appointment or by walk-in. In the former, the person learns about the SST service and contacts the service to make an appointment with a therapist. In the latter, the person literally walks into the service, completes a short intake form and usually sees a therapist immediately or after a short break. While further sessions are available in both 'by appointment' and 'walk-in' settings, the nature of the latter means that often people do not return for further therapy.

# 2

# Misconceptions about SST

## Abstract

*In the last chapter, I considered the nature of SST by discussing some of the terms that have been used when describing this way of working. In this chapter, I look at further defining the field by considering nine misconceptions that are held by some when they are first introduced to SST and by others even before they have been introduced to it! Having listed each misconception, I set out to correct it.*

## SST is a therapeutic orientation or a single way of working

In Chapter 4, I introduce the view that perhaps the best way of thinking about SST is to consider it to involve a mindset, a particular way of viewing the work that influences practice. Consequently, SST is not a therapeutic orientation in the same way as couples therapy is not a therapeutic orientation. Also, like couples therapy, SST does not involve a single way of working. Although perhaps the dominant ideas on SST have come from what I have called the 'constructive' approaches (including solution-focused therapy, collaborative therapy, narrative therapy and strengths-based therapy), SST can and has been practised by therapists from a range of other orientations (Dryden, 2019a). Suffice it to say there is no one approach to SST. It is a mindset and a way of delivering therapeutic services.

## SST is a 'cure-all'

Advocates of SST are keen to make clear that SST is best seen as occupying an important place in a range of therapy services available within an agency's therapy provision. It is not supposed to replace such services, and nobody in the SST community would argue that it should be offered to and used with everybody seeking help.

## SST is a quick fix

The term 'quick fix' means something that seems to be a fast and easy solution to a problem but is, in fact, not very good or will not last long. This is not what SST therapists attempt to do. Instead, they strive to work with clients to find a meaningful, durable solution to a problem or to help them take steps that will lead to such a solution.

## SST is used to save money

Budget holders may be attracted to SST because they see it as a way of reducing costs. In Chapter 5, I argue that SST is based on the idea that help should be provided at the point of need rather than at the point of availability. When services are restructured to provide 'at the point of need' help then it may be that money is also saved. Even if this the case, this should not be the prime reason for this way of delivering therapeutic services.

## SST restricts access to therapy

The basic idea behind SST is not to offer clients only one session but to help them get the most out of the session on the basis that it *may* be the only session that they have. It is possible to offer clients one session of therapy which is not informed by the principle of helping them get the most out of the session. To my mind, this would be the worst of both worlds – restricting the client to one session and not helping them to get the most out of the session.

In most SST services, further sessions are possible, usually booked one-at-a-time rather than, for example, booked weekly months into the future, unless this is clinically indicated. Thus, SST does not restrict access to therapy. Instead, it is tempered by the needs of all who use the service so that nobody has to wait longer than he or she needs to.

## SST is speeded-up therapy

Some people think that SST is like 'therapy speeded up' where the therapist attempts to cram a number of sessions into one session. This is not the case. In fact, if a therapist attempts to do this, it often renders SST ineffective. SST is guided by two principles: 'sooner is better' and 'less is more'. My own vulnerability as an SST therapist has been to give the client as much as possible to take away with them, but as I have learned such an approach often means that the person takes nothing away with them. As Michael Hoyt has stressed for years and again recently (Hoyt, 2018), a single session has its own process. It does not try to truncate the process of, for example, a six-session therapy into one session. The session is regarded as a whole to be complete in itself (Talmon, 1990).

## SST is the same as crisis intervention

While a single session can help people with crises, SST is not the same as crisis intervention. Thus, a person does not have to be in crisis to benefit from SST. Also, a person in crisis may need a number of sessions to resolve the crisis.

## SST is easy because it involves one session

Some therapists think that long-term therapy is complex and this may be the case. These therapists think that by contrast brief therapy is relatively easy and by extension, SST is the easiest of them all. However, I would beg to differ. If 'less is more' in SST (see above), 'less is also more difficult'. Given its brevity and focus, it is quite difficult to practise, and SST therapists require high-level thera- peutic skills.

## SST is for everyone

While SST can be helpful, it is certainly not for all clients. There are clients who want ongoing therapy – whether they need it or not – and these people would not respond well to being offered a single session even if further sessions may be available and even if a com- pelling rationale for its use has been made. Other clients want the security of an ongoing relationship with a therapist, and their clin- ical preferences should be respected.

Also, SST is not for all therapists. Some therapists believe that they can only practise therapy once they have carried out a full his- tory and case formulation. Clearly, this cannot be done in SST, and such therapists would struggle to practise when time is at a premium.

It is neither a good idea to require clients to have SST when it is not wanted, nor to mandate therapists to practise SST, particularly where their ideas and related skills are not consistent with the SST mindset (see Chapter 5). On the contrary, SST is best practised when clients see the potential in it, and therapists embrace the challenge of helping willing clients in the shortest possible period.

# 3

# People have the capacity to help themselves quickly

## Abstract

*Single-session therapy rests on the assumption that people can help themselves quickly if the conditions are in place for them to do so. If this were not the case, then SST would not be possible. In this chapter, I present an example of how someone helped themself quickly and then use this example to spell out the four significant conditions that need to be in place for someone to help themself quickly.*

## The case of Paul and his fear of heights

I got a call from Paul who discovered that I offer SST among my clinical services. He wanted to propose to his girlfriend Angela in a romantic setting, and her sister told him in confidence that it was Angela's dream to be proposed to at the top of the Eiffel Tower. This posed a problem for Paul since he had a longstanding fear of heights. He had arranged for himself and Angela to go to Paris in five days' time and was keen to propose to her during the trip in a surprise visit to the Eiffel Tower. Could I, he enquired, help him to overcome his fear of heights without using hypnosis, which he had tried before and which did not suit him. I replied that while this was a 'tall' order, if we both gave it our best shot, we would see if we could solve the problem. He agreed, and we decided to meet for a single session the next day.

At the session, it transpired that Paul was anxious about the swaying sensations he predicted he would get when in high places, along with the image of him throwing himself off wherever he was. As we explored a little further, Paul confirmed that the swaying sensations were evidence to him that he was losing control, something that he held that he could not tolerate. I asked Paul if he would like to hear my view of why he had the images of throwing himself off the high space, and he was keen to hear them. My view was that these images stemmed from Paul's intolerant attitude towards the swaying sensations and if he tolerated these sensations without liking them, then eventually they would not linger in his mind for long. Paul agreed with this view and was keen to apply what we then discussed. This was that he needed to expose himself to his swaying sensations, first on the ground and then in high places. Paul resolved to do this and spent the next two days doing so. He texted the next week telling me that he proposed to Angela at the top of the Eiffel Tower and she accepted!

## The four conditions of rapid change

In my view, for a person help themselves quickly, four conditions need to be present: (i) knowledge; (ii) a committed reason to change; (iii) preparedness to accept the costs of change if any; and (iv) taking appropriate action. As we shall see, all four conditions' ingredients were present in Paul's case, and therefore he was able to change in a short period.

### Knowledge

Knowing what to do is probably the weakest of the four conditions in accounting for rapid change. In some approaches to SST (e.g. CBT-based approaches), knowledge is crucial, while in other approaches, it is relatively unimportant and may be counterproductive (e.g. Ericksonian approaches).

For Paul, however, knowledge was significant in two respects. First, knowledge helped him to make sense of why he was having the symptoms that he was experiencing and second, it showed him what he needed to do to address his problem adequately. If you do not know what to do, then you will not do it, but knowing what to do does not mean that you are going to do it. This is why knowledge can be a key condition in facilitating rapid change but is usually insufficient.

## A committed reason to change

Having a good reason to change and being committed to the reason is core. The timeliness of the change is a central factor here too. Thus, Paul wanted to address his fear of heights, not for himself, but for his girlfriend who had always dreamed of receiving a proposal of marriage at the top of the Eiffel Tower. The time factor was that they were both going to Paris five days after he made contact with me. If he was going to propose, he had to take action promptly.

## Preparedness to accept any costs of change

Unfortunately, psychological change usually involves the person experiencing some costs. These costs may be internal (e.g. the person has to put up with some pain or discomfort to get the desired benefit), interpersonal (e.g. some of the person's relationships may suffer if they make the change), or pragmatic (the person may lose specific benefits if they change). If the person is prepared to accept such costs they will tend to change; if not, they will not. Paul had to accept internal costs if he was to address his fear of heights effectively. These costs were that he would need to tolerate the discomfort of his swaying sensations and the images of him throwing himself from high places while facing these places. Paul stated that he was prepared to accept these costs of change.

13

## Taking appropriate action

A person may meet the previous three criteria, but unless they are prepared to take action based on what they have learned when discussing these conditions with their therapist, then they probably won't change. Paul knew that to achieve his goal of proposing to Angela at the top of the Eiffel Tower, he needed first to seek out a number of high places and tolerate the swaying sensations and the images of him throwing himself off each place. He did this and only left each place when he was no longer afraid. As a result, Paul was able to go to the top of the Eiffel Tower without anxiety and proposed to Angela, a proposal which she accepted.

It is incredible sometimes what people can achieve in a very short period. Rod Temperton, the British songwriter from Cleethorpes who wrote 'Thriller' for Michael Jackson, decided with Quincy Jones, the producer, that he would write verses to be read by Vincent Price at the end of the song. Price was coming to the studio the next day at 2 pm, so Temperton gave himself six hours to do the writing and deliver it to the studio. However, he had forgotten that his British agent was coming to have a breakfast meeting which lasted until noon that day. Temperton now had two hours to write the verses and deliver them. He did so with moments to spare and the results, as anyone familiar with 'Thriller' would know, were spectacular (Pitman, 2017).

# 4

# SST is based on providing help at the point of need rather than help at the point of availability

## Abstract

*In this chapter, I compare two pathways to help, one based on providing help at the point of need and the other based on providing help at the point of availability. In looking at the assumptions underlying each pathway, it is clear that SST is based on providing help at the point of need.*

The idea of SST can often be tangled up in the minds of professionals with notions such as 'quick fix', 'flight into health, 'spontaneous remission', 'treatment dropout' and 'superficial change'. With such pejorative ideas associated with SST, it is often hard for SST therapists to get a fair hearing when presenting SST to colleagues who are not already advocates of this way of working. However, when we look at what clients say about SST services, a very different picture emerges.

## Pathways to help

If you ask clients to choose between having a single session of therapy with the promise of at least another session if needed or having ongoing therapy, probably most would choose the latter. However, if the choice was the same but put into a more realistic context, then a different answer may be forthcoming. Thus, if the question was

'Which pathway would you like to opt for, pathway 1 or pathway 2? In pathway 1, you would have a single session of therapy immediately (or with only a few days' wait) with at least another session if you needed it. In pathway 2, you would be put onto a waiting list for an assessment for ongoing therapy, and if deemed suitable you would be put onto another waiting list for actual treatment with a combined waiting time of over three months'. I guess that a significant number would opt for pathway 1.

## An example of pathway 1

This was indeed the case at the Arts University of Bournemouth (AUB) in the South of England, which had been using a six-session counselling model where all students were offered a maximum of six counselling sessions before realising that they could not sustain this service delivery in the face of growing and unsustainable waiting lists. This six-session contract was itself a reduction from the previous twelve-session contract! They had decided that they wanted to initiate some kind of SST service delivery when they sought my consultancy and training help. Eventually, they settled on what I would classify as a 'one-at-a-time' service delivery approach, which they introduced at the beginning of the 2017–18 academic year. Here, students would be seen quickly and they could book another session at the end of the first, but they could not book a series of appointments. This resulted in a slashing of the waiting list, which at the service's busiest point was only five days as compared to the many weeks' wait for an appointment when the six-session contract was in place.

Interestingly, when student opinion was canvassed, students who began their college course at the same time as the OAAT service was introduced were most appreciative of being able to have a counselling session when they needed it. By contrast, returning students who were accustomed to the six-session model complained about losing services. This shows the importance of placing SST in context when introducing it to service users and other professionals.

The voice of new students at AUB clearly indicated the importance of help being provided at the point of need rather than at the point of availability.

## *Help at the point of need*

Nobody in the helping professions would argue with the ideal that all people who require psychological assistance should be offered the help they need at the point of that need. The problem is that we live in a world of scarce resources and it is very unlikely that financial budgets will ever be provided to enable this to happen, especially in a National Health Service such as exists in the United Kingdom today. Consequently, decisions have to be made concerning how to structure services to improve access to psychological therapies. Of course, such decisions are often driven by budgetary concerns, but not exclusively. These decisions are also informed by what people believe is central to providing help to clients. In Table 4.1, I have outlined some assumptions that underly the two different ways of structuring psychological services: providing help at the point of need and at the point of availability.

As you will see from this table, the assumptions that underlie help provided at the point of need stress the importance of responding when the person seeks help, and to provide therapy from the outset rather than other services which do not involve active treatment. For example, some NHS foundation trusts provide a drop-in service under the heading 'Talking Shops'. As can be seen in the following extract,[1] the help provided in one such 'Talking Shop', while valuable, is not SST:

Our Talking Shops in Doncaster and Scunthorpe are drop-in advice and psychological therapy shops which give people the opportunity to browse information on mental health issues and gain knowledge about the therapies offered by the Trust.

Information at the shops includes prevention and self-help literature, the very latest computer-based intervention programmes,

17

**Table 4.1 Help provided at the point of need vs. at the point of availability: Some underlying assumptions**

| Help provided at the point of need | Help provided at the point of availability |
|---|---|
| • It is better to respond to client need by providing some help straightaway rather than by waiting to provide the best possible help | • It is better to have clients wait for the best possible help than to provide them with some help when they need it |
| • Providing immediate help is more important than carrying out an assessment | • Carrying out an assessment is more important than offering immediate help |
| • Therapy should start immediately. A case formulation should be carried out, if needed | • Therapy should only be carried out on the basis of a formulation of the case |
| • Therapy can be initiated in the absence of a case history | • It is important to take a case history before therapy is initiated |
| • People have the resources to make use of help provided at the point of need | • People have the resources to make use of help provided on the basis of a case formulation |
| • Sooner is better | • More is better |
| • The best way to see if a client will respond well to therapy is by offering them therapy and see how they respond | • The best way to see if a client will respond well to therapy is to offer them the most appropriate therapy based on a full assessment of their problems and on a formulation of their 'case' |

(Continued)

**Table 4.1 (Cont.)**

| Help provided at the point of need | Help provided at the point of availability |
|---|---|
| • Therapy can be initiated and risk managed if this becomes an issue | • Risk has to be properly managed before therapy is initiated |
| • Appropriate therapy length is best determined by the client | • Appropriate therapy length is best determined by the therapist |
| • When a person does not return for another session, this may well indicate that the person is satisfied with what they achieved, although it may be the case that they were dissatisfied with the help provided | • When a person does not return for another session or before they have completed their 'course of treatment', they have dropped out of this treatment and it should be regarded as a bad outcome |

as well as an opportunity for a short initial consultation with a health professional if necessary.

Reception staff and volunteers help visitors to access information and use the computers. Carers of people with mental health problems are also able to access information and local support.

People who may benefit from a course of treatment with a therapist are advised how they can access this through the available referral pathways. (This would usually include a consultation with their GP).

Once referred to the Rotherham Doncaster and South Humber NHS Foundation Trust IAPT service, our therapists can provide you with a wide range of talking therapies, which include cognitive behavioural therapy (CBT) and counselling.

I made the point at the beginning of the chapter that therapists new to SST are often sceptical about what can be achieved from a single session. However, when service users are followed-up and asked about their experiences of SST, the majority indicate that they are satisfied with the help provided (see Hoyt & Talmon, 2014a).

## *Note*

1   Originally posted on talkingsense.org, a website run by the Rotherham Doncaster and South Humber NHS Trust in conjunction with the Improving Access to Psychological Therapies (IAPT) programme: www.talkingsense.org/how-we-can-help/the-talking-shop/ (accessed 20th June 2016).

# 5

# The SST mindset

## Abstract

*In this chapter, I consider and discuss the components of what is called the therapist's SST mindset. I will also outline what I consider to be the client's SST mindset. If the client is to get the most out of the single session, then it is crucial for the therapist and client to have SST mindsets that are compatible.*

## The therapist's mindset in SST

While there are some core practices within SST which I will discuss in more detail in the second part of this book, it is constructive to consider what some in the SST community describe as the single-session mindset. An excellent overview of this mindset is provided by Jeff Young (2018: 44), which he calls an "SST informed attitude to clinical work". It is important to make clear at the outset that Young's SST mindset is held in the minds of therapists. Later, I will consider what might comprise a client-held SST mindset. From a working alliance perspective (see Chapter 13), unless both therapist and client approach SST with a similar mindset, then the latter will not get as much as they could from the work than if they do share this mindset. Indeed, the work may not even commence.

## Move forward on the 'as-if' principle

As we saw in Chapter 1, there is no universally agreed definition of SST. However, there is what I call the 'as-if' principle to which the majority of SST therapists would adhere. This describes the phenomenon where therapists approach the first session 'as if' it could be the only session they have with a client. This is the case, says Young (2018: 44), "irrespective of diagnosis, complexity or severity". That being said, this mindset includes the idea that further sessions are possible should both client and therapist agree.

## Develop an end-of-session focus

Instead of asking the client what they want to achieve by the end of *therapy*, the SST therapist, mindful that this may be the only session that they have with the client (see above), has it in mind to ask the client what they would like to achieve by the end of the *session*. This focuses the client's mind on the now rather than some unspecified time in the perhaps far-off future when therapy might end.

## Agree on a focus in the session

Once the client has specified what they would like to walk away with at the end of the session, the SST therapist negotiates with the client until they agree on a focus for the session which will help the client to achieve their goal.

**Keep on track.** Given that time is at a premium in SST and given the human tendency to drift away from an agreed focus, the therapist keeps it in mind that it is their responsibility to keep the client on track, interrupting the client if necessary but always tactfully. My own suggestion is to ask clients at the outset for permission to interrupt them should the need arise.

## Utilise client strengths

All SST therapists agree that it is crucial to help the clients to identify their strengths and apply them to the SST process both within the single session and to the application of learning after the session has ended.

## Share what might be helpful

As I will discuss in Chapter 6, SST therapists draw upon a wealth of therapeutic wisdom from a plethora of different sources. Young (2018: 45) urges SST therapists to ask themselves, "What would I want to share with this client if I never see them again?". While different therapists will have a different answer to this question, based in part on their favoured way of working, the critical point made by Young (2018) here is that any suggestions made should be put tentatively to the client for their consideration and discussion. Most SST therapists would also say that such suggestions should be based on effective strategies that the client has previously used on this and other issues and should also make use of the client's strengths and resiliency factors.

## Provide resources and utilise

Young's (2018) point about having it mind to provide clients with resources to take away with them is based on the view that the client can draw upon what the external world offers regarding resources that can help clients build upon what they gained from the session. These might include online resources, geographically close organisational resources, support resources and booklets relevant to the client's concerns.

## Clarify next steps

It is generally agreed that the client should not be left hanging at the end of SST and that definite next steps should be negotiated. My view is that the client should be encouraged to go away to reflect on the session, digest what they learned, try out a few things on the basis of this learning, let things settle and book another session if one is required. Some kind of follow-up may also be agreed at this point.

## The client's mindset in SST

Compared to the therapist's mindset in SST, there has been less written on what might be termed the client's mindset in SST. This describes the collection of ideas that clients hold about coming to therapy which, if acted on, would help them gain as much as they could from the session. However, it is possible to extract such a mindset from writings on desirable client characteristics in SST (Dryden, 2017; Talmon, 1990).

### Be ready to address the problem now

Some clients come to therapy with the idea that it will take them a long time to address their problems, with the result that it does. It is significant, therefore, for the client to have the idea that they may well be able to address their problem in one visit and be willing to join the therapist in an active alliance where both work hard together to do just that.

### Be open to and give feedback on any suggestions from the therapist

One of the components of the therapist's SST mindset, put forward by Young (2018), is the willingness to share something that the client may find helpful, but tentatively. If this can be received in an open-minded way by the client, who is then willing to voice any concerns about it rather than dismissing it out of hand or agreeing with it compliantly, then the resulting discussion can yield something perhaps more helpful than the therapist's original suggestion.

### Keep expectations realistic

As I will discuss in greater detail in the following chapter, it is vital for the client to have realistic expectations concerning what they can take from SST. The person who expects a profound shift in person-ality or quantum change (Miller & C' de Baca, 2001) after a single session is hoping for magic. Whereas, the person who hopes to get unstuck and take a few steps forward is demonstrating a realistic SST mindset.

## Be prepared to put learning into practice

When a client comes to a therapy session keen to put what they learn into practice, then this mindset will encourage them to get the most from the session, mainly if this commitment to action is ongoing.

When the client's and therapist's SST mindsets complement one another, then they demonstrate a strong working alliance in the 'views' domain, which contributes to a good outcome from the session.

**6**

# The importance of expectations in SST

### Abstract

*In this chapter, I discuss the vital role that expectations play in SST. I begin by considering clients' expectations, particularly concerning the time therapy should take, but also about what can be achieved from a single session. I then discuss the expectations held by therapists and how they can shape and be shaped by clients' expectations.*

### Clients' expectations

In this section, I will discuss clients' expectations concerning time and outcome. Constantino, Ametrano & Greenberg (2012) distinguish between two types of client expectations in psychotherapy: *treatment expectations* (concerning what will happen during therapy), including how they and their therapists will behave (role expectations), their subjective experience of therapy (process expectations), and how long treatment will last (duration expectations) and outcome expectations (concerning what they will achieve from therapy). In this chapter, I will consider clients' duration expectations and *outcome expectations*.

### Duration expectations

In an important chapter on time in brief therapy, Hoyt (1990: 115) makes the salient point that "brief therapy is defined more by an attitude than by the specific number of treatment sessions". This attitude can have a profound effect on both the therapist and the client. When considering the impact of clients' duration expectations, for example, Battino (2014) discusses hearing de Shazer (1982) talk about a research project carried out at the 'Brief Family Therapy Center' in Milwaukee on the effect of clients' expectations of the time therapy should take on their behaviour in therapy. In that study, clients were randomly told that therapists in that centre usually took either five or ten sessions to help people with their particular issue. What the researchers found was that clients in the 'five-session' treatment began doing 'significant' work in the fourth session and that clients in the 'ten-session treatment' began doing significant work in the eighth or ninth session. In commenting on this interesting finding, Battino (2014) cites the oft-quoted 'Parkinson's law of psychotherapy' (Appelbaum, 1975), which states that therapy expands and contracts to fill the time allocated to it.[1]

Thus, if clients expect therapy to last a specified period, then this would determine the duration of therapy. Before I got interested in SST, occasionally an overseas client would wish to see me for a course of therapy while they were in London. On one occasion, I agreed to see the person for five sessions over a two-week period, and that proved to be helpful to the person. On another occasion, I had much less time to see the person and could only offer one session. The client accepted the offer, worked enormously hard in that session and achieved comparatively the same benefit as the person who had five sessions. I should add that restricting time in the second case was not a deliberate strategy so that the person would work hard in the very brief time they had with me. I genuinely only had one hour. It is only now when I look back at the two scenarios that I can see clearly that each client used the time allocated to them.

## Outcome expectations

In Chapter 4, I mentioned that having realistic expectations for change was one of the features of what I called the client's SST mindset. If a client comes to therapy in a demoralised state thinking that nothing much can be achieved, then the therapist needs to address this quickly and help the client to see that change, even from a single therapy session, is possible. Otherwise, a self-fulfilling prophecy may 'kick in' and yield little or no change for the client. Alternatively, if the client thinks that they will profoundly change their personality in a single session, then disappointment will usually ensue. However, if the client thinks that change is possible and that they can begin that process in one session with the therapist's help, then this augurs well for a good outcome. The therapist helping the client to set realistic goals is usually a meaningful part of this process.

## Therapists' expectations

Rosenthal & Jacobson (1968) carried out an important piece of research on the impact of teacher expectations on pupil performance. Children, whose teachers expected them to achieve well, did, in fact, achieve more than children whose teachers did not expect them to achieve well. This was the case despite there being no other differences between the two groups of children. This occurred through teachers responding to the 'intellectual bloomers', as the first group were called, in more positive ways than to children in the other group.

There is a vast literature on the impact of therapist expectations in psychotherapy (see Constantino, Glass, Arnkoff, Ametrano & Smith, 2011). In short, and extrapolating from Rosenthal & Jacobson's (1968) findings to therapy, if a therapist thinks that the client can gain from a single session, then this will affect the therapist's behaviour in positive ways and lead to the client engaging more constructively with the process. Additionally, if the client thinks that they can gain from the single session, then their behaviour will also have a galvanising impact on the therapist who will then work harder to help the client achieve their goal.

As I said elsewhere:

*If both participants [in SST] expect change, then it is more likely to happen than if they don't. If the therapist expects that client change can be achieved from the session, but the client doesn't believe this, then the 'feel' of the work will be of the therapist pulling along a client who will resist the therapist's pace. If the client thinks that they can achieve what they want from the session and the therapist doesn't, then the 'feel' of the work will be of the client being frustrated at being held up the therapist.*

*(Dryden, 2019a: 87)*

I go on to say that, "[e]ven if both therapist and client hold realistic expectations of what the latter can achieve from SST, if the therapist pushes for change, it may not happen" (Dryden, 2019a: 88). Thus, while expectations influence the outcome of SST, other therapeutic ingredients such as pacing and working together are also primary, as I will discuss in the second part of this book.

## *Note*

1  This phenomenon also operates in other spheres of life. For example, I found as an academic that if a deadline was set six months after a piece of work was given, then most students would submit their work in the final 30 minutes of the deadline. However, if the same piece of work was due in nine months then again most students would submit their work in the final half-hour!

# 7

# SST is a fusion between what the client brings to the process and what the therapist brings to the process

## Abstract

*In this chapter, I argue that SST is a fusion of client and therapist factors, and while the therapist helping the client to use extant strengths etc. is a key idea, there is nothing to stop the therapist offering the client something new so long as this is done in a way that empowers rather than disempowers the client.*

As I argued in Chapter 5, SST is a mindset rather than a specific approach. Thus, it is possible to practise SST in a variety of different ways but to be guided by the SST mindset in doing so. In this chapter, I will discuss the idea that SST is a fusion between what clients bring to the process and what therapists bring to the process.

## Client empowerment

Hoyt et al. (2018a: 14–15) note that the concept of 'client empowerment' is a key feature of approaches to SST such as solution-focused, collaborative, narrative therapy and strengths-based therapy (which I call here the 'constructive' approaches). These approaches argue that what clients bring to the work is the most significant contributory factor to the outcome of SST and that these factors include the following.

## Internal strengths

Part of the therapist's SST mindset is the view that all clients have internal strengths that they have either overlooked or lost touch with, which potentially they can bring to the SST process.

## Values

When people are connected to their values, i.e. their judgments of what is important to them in their lives, then this can have a profound effect on what they can achieve from SST.

## Previous attempts to solve the problem

It is very likely that the client has attempted to solve their problem before coming to SST. To help empower the client, the therapist will help them to identify and capitalise on those attempts that have had some positive impact in the past and that they can use in the future.

## Successful attempts to deal with other problems

When a client seeks therapy, it is likely that their focus will be on the problem that they have not solved. However, it is probable that they have solved other problems and it is empowering for them to focus on what they did to bring about change in these other areas and see that they can perhaps use these to solve the current problem.

## Helping others

It is also likely that the client has had the experience of helping other people, perhaps even with the problem for which they are seeking help. Reminding the person of this and encouraging them to consider applying the helping factor(s) to their current problem is part of the empowerment process.

## Being helped by others

It is also likely that the client has had the experience of being helped by others in the past either within therapy or outside. When the helping ingredients have been identified, then the information may help the person apply them to themself, or it may help the therapist to help the client in a similar way.

## Role models

A client may be inspired by people whom they admire. Having a client identify a role model relevant to the problem for which they are seeking help can accelerate the change process.

## Guiding principles

My mother used to say to me, "Son, if you don't ask, you won't get". I often refer to this 'guiding principle' in my mind, if I am unsure about asking for something as a prelude to action. Helping the client to identify a relevant guiding principle can provide a significant impetus to change.

## External resources

I distinguish between strengths which are internal to the person and resources which are external to the person. Such resources include people who can support the person during the change process and organisations which can provide help, information and support. The adage which states, 'only you can do it, but you do not have to do it alone' is particularly apt here (Lonergan, 2012). Helping the person to see that they can utilise such resources is significant when the contact between therapist and client is so short.

## *Therapist contributions*

Therapists' contributions to SST are dependent on how they view the work. As I will discuss in Chapter 23, there are three major traditions in SST: constructive, active-directive and pluralistic. Perhaps the predominant tradition in SST is the constructive one, and thus I will emphasise it is this section. Hoyt et al. (2018b) argue that the major role of constructive therapists in SST is to help clients to identify and apply to the SST process the factors that I reviewed in the previous section. As they have eloquently put it, the role of the therapist in SST is to "use their expertise primarily to help clients better use their own expertise" (Hoyt et al., 2018b: 15). They contrast constructive approaches with approaches "in which change is primarily brought about by the therapist forming an opinion about what is wrong... and then proceeding to provide what the therapist discerns to be the needed remedy". I will refer to these here as 'active-directive' approaches and will discuss them more fully in Chapter 23, in perhaps a more 'constructive' way.[1] There is a third growing tradition in SST that I call the pluralistic tradition. This tradition prioritises the client's viewpoint and advocates a both/and rather than an either/or approach to practice. Pluralistic practitioners are happy to utilise the strengths of the constructive and active-directive traditions without worrying too much about their different theoretical underpinnings.

### *Sharing expertise vs being the expert*

I see SST as a fusion between what the client brings to the process and what the therapist brings to the process. The SST therapist should work to identify a whole host of client factors and encourage the clients to use them in the service of their goal. However, why should the therapist not *also* claim the freedom to ask the client if they are interested in hearing something that the client may not have thought of which may shed light on their problem and how to tackle it? Moreover, is it such a crime if this knowledge stems from the collective wisdom that underpins the therapist's own orientation?

The therapist can show and use their expertise without coming across as 'the expert' in a way that disempowers the client. In short, in SST, it is possible for the therapist to *both* share expertise *and* empower the client.

### Note

1   Pun intended!

# 8

## SST challenges therapists' cherished beliefs about therapy and change

### Abstract

*Whenever I give a presentation or workshop on single-session therapy, I warn the audience that what I have to say may challenge their valued ideas about therapy and psychological change. In doing so, I call upon them to listen to me with as much of an open mind as they can muster. Despite this, many therapists find themselves resisting SST. In this chapter, I consider and discuss some of the therapists' beliefs that SST challenges.*

### Therapists need to build a sound therapeutic relationships with clients, and these take time to develop

It is clear from a number of reviews that the quality of therapeutic relationships is a vital variable in accounting for a good therapeutic outcome (e.g. Lambert, 2013). While it may be the case that with specific clients it takes time to develop a sound working alliance, this is not universally so, and this latter notion challenges the beliefs of many therapists.

It is part of the SST mindset that therapists can develop a good working relationship with clients quickly and they do so by i) taking seriously the client's presenting problem rather than considering that it hides the 'real' problem; ii) negotiating with the client a realistic goal for the session that relates to the presenting problem; iii) getting down to work quickly and inviting the client to do the same; and iv) showing that they are keen to provide help. Simon, Imel, Ludman & Steinfeld's (2012) research showed that clients benefitting from SST report a strong working alliance with their therapists while clients not benefitting from SST report a weak alliance with their therapists. Such research shows that it is entirely possible to form a good working relationship with clients quickly.

## *More is better*

The problem with the way therapists are trained is that such training most often centres on therapy that lasts much longer than the research indicates that many clients want. Thus, it is generally accepted that the modal number of sessions per treatment is 'one' internationally (Hoyt & Talmon, 2014a; Hoyt et al., 2018a). However, training courses rarely train students to offer SST and this, I believe, teaches them, albeit implicitly, that 'more is better'. However, research does not support this idea. Thus, Lambert's (2013) review showed that the greatest amount of change occurs early in treatment rather than later and the amount of change clients experience diminishes as the number of sessions they have increases. My view is that if training courses train students to offer their clients SST and very brief forms of therapy, *as well as* longer-term therapy, the idea that 'more is better' would not be as prevalent as it currently is.

## *Subjective measures of disturbance and change are flawed, and therefore it is best to judge change objectively rather than from the client's subjective view*

Quite rightly, when psychotherapy is studied scientifically, it is important to use objective measures of change as well as subjective measures. However, in my view, there is too much reliance on the former as opposed to the latter when listening to clients report on what they received from SST. When clients seek help, it is because they are in subjective distress and not because of their score on an objective measure of disturbance. Just because SST clients may not have objectively made a 'clinically significant change' from a single session, the fact that they claim to have benefitted from it and are pleased with the service that they received should not be dismissed. Yes, subjective measures of disturbance are flawed, but so are human beings, so let's listen to what they have to say and if they say that they have benefitted from SST, let's not dismiss it. After all, we did not dismiss it when they subjectively claimed to be disturbed when seeking help.

## *Psychologically meaningful change happens slowly and gradually*

As discussed above, professionals often distinguish between change that is clinically significant change and change that is not. Clinically significant change occurs when someone moves outside the range of the dysfunctional population or within the range of the functional population (Jacobson, Follette & Revenstorf, 1984). Even when people acknowledge that therapeutic change does take place in SST, they dismiss it by saying that such change is not clinically significant. For clinically significant change, it is claimed, happens slowly and gradually. However, Hayes, Laurenceau, Feldman, Strauss & Cardaciotto (2007) have shown that while clinically significant change can be gradual and linear, this is not universally the case and that such change can occur quite quickly. It is the *possibility* of a meaningful change occurring in a short period in SST that challenges the commonly held idea that real change only occurs slowly and gradually.

Also, as noted above, who decides what is meaningful change and what isn't? Just because objectively the change a person makes in SST does not meet the criterion of clinically significant or meaningful change does not mean that subjectively it is not meaningful to the person.

### *SST is not suitable for clients facing complex problems*

One of the most common questions asked by therapists first exposed to SST concerns the suitability of SST: "Who is SST suitable for and for whom is it not suitable?" I discuss this issue in Chapter 10.

Many SST therapists note that people with complex problems often seek simple solutions to these complex problems and are satisfied when they find such solutions within an SST framework (Hoyt et al., 2018a). Hoyt & Talmon (2014a: 503) reviewed a number of studies that show that "the efficacy of SSTs is not restricted only to 'easy' cases, but can have far-reaching effects in many areas, including treatment of alcohol and substance abuse as well as self-harming behavior".

# 9

# What can be achieved from SST

## Abstract

*In this chapter, I consider what can be achieved from SST. I begin by making the obvious point that, in all probability, one session will not bring about quantum change. On the other hand, what a single session can do, among other things is to help a person get unstuck, to change their behaviour and see its impact on another, to face and process adversity and to leave a situation that is problematic for the person and where change is unlikely to happen.*

## What probably cannot be achieved from SST

There is a concept in psychology known as quantum change which shows that meaningful change can occur in a concise period both inside and outside psychotherapy. Quantum change refers to a sudden, dramatic and enduring change that affects a broad range of emotion, cognition and behaviour (Miller & C' de Baca, 2001). Perhaps the most well-known example of quantum change is Scrooge in Charles Dickens' short story, *A Christmas Carol*. Scrooge goes to bed on Christmas Eve, a curmudgeonly, miserly old man who hates Christmas, is generally nasty to everyone he knows and whose only love is money. During the night he is visited by three spirits, the ghosts of Christmas past, Christmas present and Christmas yet to come. These spirits show Scrooge to himself in an increasingly negative light culminating with his death mourned by nobody and whose grave is neglected. Scrooge promises to change to avoid this fate and does so. When he wakes up, he begins to treat everyone with kindness, generosity and compassion, embodying the spirit of Christmas.

I have told this story to indicate what probably cannot be achieved with SST. Indeed, if a client sets this kind of change as an end-of-session goal the SST therapist, while not dismissing quantum change as an aspiration, would probably encourage the person instead to identify a sign that they had begun the journey towards this end.

## What probably can be achieved from SST

Having outlined what probably can't be changed in SST, let me now concentrate on what probably can be achieved. The following is a sample of what can realistically be achieved.

### Getting unstuck

Quite often people come to therapy because they are stuck in a self-defeating pattern. Sometimes people unwittingly maintain their problems due to the fixed nature of their attempts to solve it. It is as if their car is stuck in snow and the more they try to spin its wheels to free it from the snow, the more stuck the car gets. Helping a client to get unstuck is a viable goal in SST. This can be done in a number of ways.

**Doing something different.** One of the ways of helping a client to get unstuck is to have them consider doing something different. This can help to break the vicious cycle that has developed where unsuccessful attempts to change lead to problem maintenance and to increased use of the unsuccessful change attempt. It is some-times sufficient that when the person takes one or two steps in a healthier direction, they sow the seeds for a virtuous cycle of change where new responses lead to more favourable responses from the environment.

## Changing behaviour to influence others

People often come to therapy with the hidden (and sometimes not so hidden) agenda of changing someone with whom they have difficulty. While a change in another person is not within the control of the client, it may be in their sphere of influence. To this end, it may be useful to discuss with the client that the best way of bringing about a change in another is to bring about a change in oneself first. While this may mean a change in attitude, the only way the other person will be aware of this is by seeing it in the client's behaviour. So, as I often say to a client in SST: "If you want to have a better relationship with the other, show them this by making a change in your behaviour so that they can see this".

## Dealing with adversity in more constructive ways

The foundation of my own SST practice is Rational Emotive Behaviour Therapy (Dryden, 2019b). My experience is that when a person seeks therapy, it is because they experience difficulty in dealing with recurring adversity (e.g. loss, failure, criticism). They may have tried to help themself deal with such adversities through avoidance and positive reframing, for example, but while such strategies afford people immediate relief, they do not help them face the adversity and process it in ways that help them going forward.

I have carried out many what I call 'very brief therapeutic conversations', which are one-off demonstration sessions of the way I work held in front of an audience (see Dryden, 2018a). The person's emotions give a clue to the type of adversity that they are struggling with (see Table 9.1).

In my view, it is possible for the SST therapist to help the client deal with the adversity by facing it and processing it in ways that mean that they do not have to avoid it in the future or to put an unrealistic 'spin' on it. How they do this is going to be dependent on a number of factors, including their favoured therapeutic orientation and the client's experience of dealing with adversities, related to their problem or in general. I find that when I encourage an SST

**Table 9.1 Common Adversities and Problematic Emotions**

| Adversity | Problematic Emotions |
|---|---|
| • Threat | Anxiety |
| • Loss<br><br>• Failure<br><br>• Undeserved plight (self or other) | Depression |
| • Moral code violation (commission or omission)<br><br>• Hurting others | Guilt |
| • Falling very short of ideal<br><br>• Others negatively evaluate self | Shame |
| • Self is more invested in the relationship than is the other | Hurt |
| • Rule violation<br><br>• Threat to self-esteem<br><br>• Frustration<br><br>• Being treated with disrespect | Problematic anger |
| • Other poses threat to one's relationship | Problematic jealousy |
| • Other has something that self prizes but does not have | Problematic envy |

client to face and process the relevant adversity, they do emerge from this work with a different, more helpful perspective on the adversity and what it means to them and about them.

**Leaving troublesome circumstances.** Sometimes a client comes to therapy with the goal of bringing about change in a troublesome set of circumstances or accepting these circumstances. An alternative that should be discussed with the client is to leave the circumstance when it is clear that the person has already made numerous attempts to change it and to accept it. This was the case with Martha who was in an unsatisfying job with a boss who was 'allergic' to change, as she put it. She wanted some guidance about how she could bring him into the modern world or to accept her plight. I asked her why she was flogging a dead horse. Here is the relevant dialogue:

> *Windy:* Why not leave?
> *Martha:* Can I do that?
> *Windy:* What does your contract say?
> *Martha:* I have to give a month's period of notice.
> *Windy:* So you have answered your own question.
> *Martha:* But what will happen to the company?
> *Windy:* It will go into liquidation, the second you leave.
> *Martha:* Very funny. I get your point.
> *Windy:* I haven't made a point.
> *Martha:* You are saying that I think I am the one keeping the company afloat.
> *Windy:* No, I'm not.
> *Martha:* That is stupid. I don't need to do that. I'm going to hand in my notice. Thanks.
> *Windy:* I haven't done anything.

I got an email from Martha five weeks later thanking me for giving her the courage to leave.

# 10

# The 'client criteria' question

## Abstract

*In this chapter, I consider the oft-asked question concerning client indications and contra-indications. I present a variety of views on this question including some client data, although we need to know more about this question from the client perspective.*

When I give presentations and training courses in SST, the most frequently asked question concerns which clients benefit from SST and which don't. While this question is reasonable, it is asked from the perspective of the therapist as if the therapist's opinion is the only one that matters. However, one of the guiding principles of SST is that the client's view should be prioritised. It seems from the literature that clients tell us that they value the opportunity to come for one therapy session and not to return if they have got what they wanted (Hoyt & Talmon, 2014a). While that might be the end of the matter, in my view it is important to consider both the therapist's perspective and the client's when addressing what I call the 'client criteria' question.

## Therapists' views on the 'client criteria' question

When we consider therapists' views on the 'client criteria' question, there seems to be two perspectives. The first perspective is that there are criteria concerning for which clients SST is indicated and for which clients it is not indicated. The second perspective is that there are no such criteria. This perspective is likely to be articulated by SST therapists who work in walk-in services.

## Yes to criteria

When therapists adopt a criteria-based approach to SST, they tend to outline a long list of indications and contra-indications. An example of this approach is outlined in Table 10.1(for indications) and Table 10.2 (for contra-indications).

## No to criteria: SST is open to all

Two groups of SST therapists tend to be against adopting a criteria-based approach to SST. The first is what I call the 'SST-embedded' group and the second is the 'walk-in' therapy group.

**The SST-embedded group.** An example of the SST-embedded group is Young's approach (2018: 48–49), whose response to the question concerning who is suitable to SST and who is not is as follows:

> We believe the best response to this question is to avoid having to answer it by embedding SST in the service system so that clients can return if they want to. Embedding SST into the service system so that all services the organization normally provides are available following an initial session, conducted as if it may be the last, allows the practitioner and the organization to avoid the 'difficult if not impossible' decision of who is suitable and who is not suitable for a 'one-off' session. For many therapists and some managers, the assumption that clients facing complex problems require 'deep' change which can only occur in long-term work is powerful and entrenched. The SST literature continues to build data to challenge this assumption.

**The walk-in therapy group.** The second group of SST therapists who do not advocate a criteria-based approach to SST are those who work in a walk-in therapy service. By its nature, walk-in therapy offers therapy to whoever needs it and uses the service. Only focused risk assessment is carried out by such therapists, and even if clients

**Table 10.1 Client indications for SST**

| Type of problems | • People with ordinary emotional problems of living |
|---|---|
| | • People with relationship issues at home and at work |
| | • People with procrastination and other forms of lack of self-discipline |
| | • People who are 'stuck' and need some help to get 'unstuck' and move on |
| | • People with 'clinical' problems, but who are ready to tackle a 'non-clinical problem'. For example, someone who has a personality disorder, but who wants help with interview anxiety |
| | • People with meta-emotional problems (e.g. shame about being anxious) |
| | • People who require prompt and focused crisis management |
| | • People facing 'life dilemmas' |
| | • People having to make an important imminent decision |
| | • People who are finding it difficult to adjust to life in some way |
| The readiness of the client | • People ready to take care of business now and whose problem is 'non-clinical', but amenable to a single-session approach. This problem will become 'clinical' if not dealt with |
| | • People ready to take care of business now and whose problem is 'clinical', but amenable to a single-session approach. One-session treatment for simple phobias (Davis III et al., 2012) or SST for panic disorder (Reinecke et al., 2013) are two examples of this |

(Continued)

Table 10.1 (Cont.)

| Issues related to therapy | • People who are open to therapy, but want to try it first before committing themselves |
|---|---|
| | • People seeking advice on how therapy would tackle their own problem |
| | • People who are reluctant and are only prepared to commit to one therapy session |
| | • People who are only in 'town' for a short period and need some help in that town |
| | • People who are volunteering for a demonstration session before an audience (e.g. Dryden, 2018a) |
| | • People who are volunteering for a videotaped demonstration session (Gloria) |
| | • Clients in therapy who are seeking a second opinion (or their therapists are) |
| | • Clients in ongoing therapy who want brief help with a problem with which their therapist can't or won't help them |
| | • Therapy trainees who want to find out what it is like to have therapy from a different perspective |
| Other issues | • People who view therapy as providing intermittent help across the life cycle |
| | • People with self-development or coaching goals |
| | • People who want some prophylactic assistance |

#### Table 10.2 Contra-indications for SST

- *Those who request ongoing therapy.* If someone wants ongoing therapy, they are disinclined to consider SST even though they could benefit from it.

- *Those who need ongoing therapy.* People who have many complex problems are likely to need a lot more therapy than can be provided by SST.

- *Clients who have many vague complaints and can't be specific.* SST offers the most to people who are able to identify and focus on a specific problem and is probably not indicated for those who find doing this very difficult.

- *Where the client finds it difficult to develop a therapeutic relationship quickly.* SST does require that the therapist and client develop a relationship quickly. When the client finds this very difficult, then SST is probably not indicated.

- *Where the client is likely to feel abandoned by the therapist.* Not only does SST call upon the client to form a relationship quickly with their therapist, but it also requires them to detach from that relationship equally quickly. When this is difficult for the client, then again SST is probably not indicated.

are at risk, they are still offered help within the single-session, walk-in paradigm. Such therapists agree with Young who says that it is rarely possible to predict who will and will not benefit from SST.

### Clients' views on the 'client criteria' question

In my book, *Very Brief Therapeutic Conversations* (Dryden, 2018a), I report on the problems that 245 people who volunteered for a brief 30-minute conversation tended to raise during that conversation (see Table 10.3). As can be seen from Table 10.3, 42 people were classified as presenting 'other emotional problems'. Table 10.4 provides a closer examination of the nature of such problems.

**Table 10.3 Themes discussed in Very Brief Therapeutic Conversations (VBTCs) by category**

| Theme category | Total |
|---|---|
| Anxiety & phobia | 49 |
| Problems with procrastination | 39 |
| Anger problems | 27 |
| Self-esteem problems | 27 |
| Problems with uncertainty | 25 |
| Relationships problems | 22 |
| Problems with lack of control | 14 |
| Other emotional problems | 42 |
| **Totals** | **245** |

(Dryden, 2018a)

**Table 10.4 Themes raised by volunteers in the theme category: Other emotional problems**

| | |
|---|---|
| Guilt | 13 |
| Hurt | 11 |
| Shame | 7 |
| Jealousy | 3 |
| Problem with responsibility | 3 |
| Envy | 2 |
| OCD | 2 |
| Avoidance of negative feelings | 1 |
| **Other emotional problems: Total** | **42** |

(Dryden, 2018a)

This shows what one group of clients thinks it is appropriate to bring up in a SST setting. We need to find out more about what problems clients think they can bring to therapy that lasts for a session so that we can get a fuller understanding of clients' perspectives on the 'client criteria' question.

11

# What makes good SST therapists

## Abstract

*If not all clients benefit from SST, then not all therapists are suited to single-session work. In this chapter, I list and discuss several qualities that it is desirable for a therapist to have and/or demonstrate for them to be a good SST therapist, in my view. The more of these qualities the therapist has and/or shows, the better they will be at delivering SST services.*

## Having and demonstrating an enthusiasm for SST

While SST requires the therapist to develop and implement a good many skills, my view is that it is fundamental that the therapist is enthusiastic about single-session work. They need to have faith that they and their client can work together to help the client to get unstuck and move on with their life. They also need to enjoy the work and the challenge that it affords. I personally find SST an energising way of working and it gives me the chance to be creative. However, above all, the SST therapist needs to communicate their enthusiasm to the client while being mindful that there are other ways of working as well.

## Laying the foundations for SST

Sometimes a client seeks out SST because they think they only need one session. This will be the case whether they are seeking SST by appointment or by walk-in. Also, sometimes a client has not given much thought to the likely duration of therapy. They may never have heard of SST, and therefore they will have had no reason to think that it may be useful for them. In all these situations and perhaps others too, it is important for the therapist to discuss with the client what SST has to offer and why the person may find it useful. This, of course, is with the usual proviso that further sessions are available if required. If the therapist lays the foundations for SST well, then they can both get down to business and address the client's issue there and then.

## Expressing themself with clarity throughout the process

Since time is at a premium in SST, the therapist can utilise the time that they and their client have at their disposal by communicating clearly. In my view, it is better to err on the side of simplicity over complexity but to do so without patronising the client. Without becoming obsessive about doing so, periodically, it is valuable to ask the client to put into their own words any substantive points that the therapist wants the client to grasp.

There may be key terms that the client and therapist use where it is crucial that they have a shared meaning of the term. Notably, where these terms are easily misunderstood, the therapist should make clear at the outset what they mean when they use the term. 'Acceptance' is one such term. I have learned that it saves time for me to clarify at the outset what I mean by the term if the client uses it or I want to use it.

## Creating and maintaining an agreed therapeutic focus

Most SST therapists will consider it a job well done if a client takes away one thing that will make a significant difference to their life. If this is to be done, then the therapist will probably have to help the client create and maintain an agreed therapeutic focus. Such a focus incorporates the client's concern and realistic goal.

To do this, the good SST therapist both checks with the clients that they are both on the right track and is able to interrupt the client with tact when the client begins to wander away from the agreed focus. See Chapter 22 for a more detailed discussion of this point.

## Maintaining the client's active involvement during the SST process

Anybody who has watched an excellent SST therapist at work will have seen a person who is able to be active themself while helping the client to maintain active involvement in the process as well. It is easy to fall prey to two errors as an SST therapist in this respect. The first error concerns the therapist failing to be sufficiently involved themself, which results in the client wandering from issue to issue without sufficient focus. The second error concerns the therapist being over-involved in the process, which results in the client adopting a complementary passive stance in the session. Guiding a middle course enables both therapist and client to work together in active harmony.

## Developing and maintaining a good pace in the session

While the SST therapist's contribution is vital in SST, most people would say that the client's contribution is central. However, a good outcome depends on them working together, but at a pace that will produce a good outcome. In this respect, I like to think that the therapist is like an accomplished pacemaker in a race which the client needs to win. The pacemaker ensures that the race is run at a pace which is not too quick to prevent the client from burning out towards the end and not too slow to prevent other runners from winning. However, it is also crucial that the pacemaker does not win

53

the race. Instead, he or she needs to bring the client along with them so that the client passes them before the end to win the race.

If the session is very speedy, then the client will not process matters sufficiently and may end up confused, and if it is too slow, then time will have run out before anything meaningful has been achieved. A good pace facilitates client processing and increases the chances that a meaningful conclusion will be reached, and a good SST therapist has the skills and sense of timing to help the client in both respects.

## Looking for and working well with clients' strengths[1]

Most therapists in the SST community consider that one of the key ingredients of a good outcome is the extent to which the therapist can help the client to identify and reconnect with their strengths in a meaningful way so that the client can use these in the construction and execution of an agreed solution to their problem. A focus on just 'what is wrong' will not achieve this. Good SST therapists look for clients' strengths in their narrative and guide them to use them at critical moments in the SST process.

## Co-creating a solution to the client's problem

Put simply, when the client comes to therapy with a problem, the good SST therapist helps them to set a goal and find a solution to the problem which enables the client to move towards the goal. In this respect, by 'solution' I mean anything that the client does to render the previous problem non-problematic and move them closer to the goal.

The good SST therapist can work with the client to co-create a solution with the client that the latter can practise in the session and implement after the session. SST services which specialise in family work often utilise a team of observing therapists as well as the participating therapist(s) (see chapters in Hoyt & Talmon,

2014b and Hoyt et al., 2018b). At an opportune moment towards the end of the session, the participating therapist(s) will take a break and consult with the therapy team where specific solutions will be discussed so that one or more can be taken back into the room to be processed with the family. SST therapists who work by themselves sometimes do this too to give themself thinking time. However, no matter which 'solution' is taken back into the room, it is good practice in SST that any solution that the client takes forward into their life is one to which they have actively signed up, if not co-created. The good SST therapist ensures that the latter happens whenever possible (see Chapter 26).

## Ending with hope

I have argued earlier in this chapter that getting the single session off to a good start is a characteristic of the good SST therapist. So is bringing the session to a suitable end. A good ending in SST is one where there are no loose ends, the work done in the session has been adequately summarised by the client (preferably), the therapist or both, the client has a clear idea where to go from here and the position on the possibility of future help has been made clear. The SST therapist who does all this and does it while engendering a sense of hope in the client that what has been done in the session can make a real difference to the person's life is a good SST therapist (see Chapter 28).

## Note

1   By strengths here, I mean all those client variables that I discussed in Chapter 7.

# 12

# For better or for worse: Context matters

## Abstract

*In this chapter, I consider the importance of context on SST. I first argue that SST is best practised within a setting which provides help at the point of need rather than help at the point of availability. I then consider other conducive organisational factors to the development of SST services.*

In the previous chapter, I considered several qualities of good SST therapists. However, no matter how talented an SST therapist may be, if that person works in a context that is not conducive to the practice of effective SST, then such talent is likely to be wasted. On the other hand, if the context in which the therapist works is conducive to the practice of SST, this context enables the therapist to enable the client to get the most out of the session.

## Conducive pathways

In Chapter 4, I argued that SST is best practised when it is embedded in a service that offers clients help at the point of need rather than help at the point of availability, and I refer the reader to that chapter for a detailed discussion of this issue. Suffice it to say, SST thrives in agencies where help is offered at the point of need (such as walk-in clinics) and struggles in agencies where help is provided only at the point of availability. Thus, it is not a good idea for an agency to set up an SST service where clients for SST would have to go on a long waiting list.[1] If a service is thinking of offering SST, its key personnel need to consider what changes the agency needs to make to offer clients help at the point of need.

Young (2018) presents research that details the fact that in a three-year period in community counselling centres in Victoria, Australia, 42% of clients attended for one session, 18% for two sessions and 10% for three sessions. The greater the number of sessions, the fewer the number of clients who attended them. This shows that while an agency may be organised to allow for the possibility that clients may only attend once, that agency needs to offer other services as well. As Young (2018) says, he wants to offer an excellent service to the 42% of clients that attend only once and to the 58% who attend more than once.

## Embedded SST

Unless an organisation only offers SST (e.g. a walk-in service which does nothing else apart from offering this kind of help), then SST needs to be integrated with an agency's other services. In doing so, it will be and will be seen to be an integral part of the total services on offer. When this happens, then the SST service will make and receive referrals from other services, and over time it will become embedded into the agency's overall provision. To facilitate this, all interested therapists should contribute to SST, and SST therapists should contribute to the other services.

Another model in which SST is embedded within an agency's provision is where everyone who is seen is considered to be a candidate for SST and where a decision about this is made after the session, where the client has had time to digest and put into practice learnings from the first (and perhaps only) session. When the phone call occurs, if further sessions are requested, they are offered (see Young, 2018). As Young notes, knowing that further help is a phone call away allows clients to be 'held' and rely on their resources more.

### Service care

Young (2018) has made the point that it is one thing for SST thinking and services to be introduced into an agency and sit along-side, shape and be shaped by existing services, it is another thing for SST to thrive in this context. As Young (2018: 41) notes:

> …if an organization does not keep SST alive with ongoing activities such as evaluation, research, and/or reflective supervisory practices, and if it is not embedded in policy, core practice and key processes, SST-inspired service delivery is lucky to survive beyond five years…. This is especially likely if key supporters of the approach leave the organization.

In other words, the service in which SST therapists work needs to care for the professional well-being of its staff so that therapists can maintain enthusiasm for working in an SST-inspired environment so that they continue to be creative in its application.

### Note

1   There is a difference between the situation where clients seek SST before attending a clinic and one where it transpires that they decided to attend one time.

# 13

# The importance of the working alliance

## Abstract

*In this chapter, I use the updated four-component working alliance framework to shed light on the SST process. I argue that when the client and therapist have a robust and collaborative bond, share similar views of facets of this process, negotiate realistic client goals and work together to find a solution that facilitates goal attainment, then there will tend to be a good outcome from the meeting.*

In my opinion, one of the most useful ideas in psychotherapy is Bordin's (1979) concept of the working alliance. According to Bordin (1979), the working alliance is comprised of three components: bonds, goals and tasks. Later, I added a fourth component, views (Dryden, 2006, 2011). In this chapter, I will use the updated working alliance framework to show how therapists can help clients get the most out of the first and perhaps the only session that they may have.

## Bonds

Bonds refer to the interconnectedness between therapist and client. There are a number of ways of understanding this interconnectedness. I will discuss two such ways: the role of the 'core conditions' in SST and the importance of developing a collaborative relationship.

## Core conditions

Rogers (1957), in a seminal article, spelt out a number of conditions that clients need to experience from their therapists if they are to gain from therapy. These 'core conditions', as they are popularly known, have undergone revision over the years, but are widely known as empathy, respect and genuineness.

### Empathy

Time is of the essence in SST. Given this, while the SST therapist needs to create space for the client to express themself, this space needs to be limited to one issue which, if resolved, will make a difference to the client's life. Within this space, it is vital for the client to experience the therapist's understanding of their struggles with the problematic issue. What I call 'empathy with a twist' is the therapist conveying an understanding of the client's struggles plus communicating a sense of hope that things could be different.

### Respect

When a therapist shows a client respect in SST, they communicate that the client is a fallible human being with strengths and weaknesses and they can use the former to help with their problem/ issue. Also, the SST therapist shows respect to the client by placing the client's choice, self-determination and empowerment centre stage in the change process.

At a more practical level, SST therapists sometimes need to interrupt clients to help them keep on track. Many therapists find doing so tricky given their prior training not to interrupt their clients' flow. One way of interrupting a client which shows respect for that client is to give a rationale for interrupting them and asking permission to do so.

## Genuineness

Being honest and giving authentic responses to a client indicate the therapist's wish to have a real relationship with the client in SST. Nowhere is this more prevalent than in Young's 'No Bullshit Therapy' – NBT (see Findlay, 2007). Here is what Young (2018: 55) says about his approach:

> NBT is enacted by creating a context where a therapist (and client) can be honest and direct, where the therapist can challenge from a good and caring place, can marry honesty and directness with warmth and care, and promote transparency and reduce obfuscation by avoiding jargon….Creating transparency in keeping with the philosophy of SST with mandated clients may look like stating how you prefer to work and seeking the client's response ("I like to be pretty upfront and direct; how does that fit with you?"), rather making the assumption that the client wants to collaborate with you.

## *Collaboration*

While mandated clients probably won't collaborate in SST, most clients have chosen to seek therapy and will collaborate with their therapist. The collaborative bond involves the following features:

- client-directed, but with the therapist sharing any concerns about the direction
- explicit negotiation of problems and/goals
- joint negotiation of a therapeutic focus
- working together to find a solution
- SST is a fusion between what the client brings to the process and what the therapist brings to the process (see Chapter 7)
- explicit negotiation about further help if needed and an agreed pathway for clients to use, if necessary
- negotiation about follow-up – if it is to occur and if so, when.

## Views

The 'views' component of the working alliance concerns the ideas that both participants hold about salient ideas of the SST process. The important point about these ideas is that the therapist and client end up by agreeing on their respective views even if they may hold different ideas at the outset.

In my opinion, there are three main areas where client and therapist need to have such agreement.

### Views on the service

I think that it is crucial that the client and therapist agree on what SST means for them in the particular situation that they are in. Does it mean only one session and that is it, or can the client have further sessions if they want to? If they request and are offered further help, are these sessions to be booked one at a time (as in OAAT Therapy) or can the client book for a series of sessions?

### Views on the problem and what accounts for it

If an SST therapist works with a client's problem, rather than a solution, then it is vital that they have an agreed understanding of the client's problem and what accounts for it. This is the case whether the therapist shares their professional understanding of the client's problem or whether the therapist elicits the client's view on the same problem. If they do not share a negotiated view of the problem, they may end up working at cross-purposes.

### Views on therapy for the problem

It is also vital that the client and therapist have a joint understanding about how this problem can best be tackled. If not, they will again be working at cross-purposes, and the session will not be fully utilised. When solutions are discussed, it is crucial that the solution is negotiated and that both can see that it has the potency to help the client to achieve their goal, if implemented.

In family-oriented SST, the sessions are often watched by an auxiliary observing team whose primary purpose is to arrive at a solution that the family is likely to implement which will help them to achieve their goals, and to suggest this to the therapist who takes a break from the session to meet with the observing team. Here, if such a solution is to 'work', first, all three parties need to agree that this is likely to be the case.

## Goals

All therapy is purposive, and this is especially the case with SST. What is specific to SST with respect to goals is that the client is asked to specify a goal for the end of the session (e.g. "If at the end of the session you thought that you got what you were hoping for, what would that be?") rather than a goal for the end of treatment. In SST, it is probably better for specific goals to be negotiated than general ones. However, if the latter is agreed, it is paramount that both client and therapist are clear about how they will both know if these goals are achieved. However, it is useful to recognise that in SST, the therapist will, in most cases, not know if the client has achieved their goal until and if a follow-up session is carried out.

The critical point about goals from a working alliance perspective is that the client and therapist agree on the client's goals so that they can work together to achieve them. If not, the single session has the quality of the client resisting the efforts of the therapist to take them in a direction to which they have not agreed, however 'healthy' such a goal may be.

## Tasks

Tasks are activities carried out by both client and therapist that are in the service of the client's goals. Again, from a working alliance perspective, it is vital for the client and therapist to have an understanding of one another's tasks, either explicitly or implicitly, and agree that the execution of these tasks is a useful way forward.

In Chapter 11, I argued that a solution is a response to a problem that helps the client to achieve their goal. As I pointed out earlier in this chapter, it is crucial for the therapist and client to agree on the nature of the solution. Here, it is vital for the client to see that they can execute the solution and that doing so will help them achieve their goal.

As I will discuss in Chapter 27, it can be valuable for the client to practise the chosen solution with the therapist in the session before using it in outside life. When this is done, the more the client believes that they can carry out the task and that it will be useful for them to do so, the more the likely it is that they will do it.

After therapy ends, the client is left to implement the solution themself without direct therapeutic help. The client can be prepared to do this if the therapist can guide them through this process using imagery to do so.

## Conclusion

The working alliance framework is a useful way of thinking about the practice of SST from a general point of view that can be used by therapists from different orientations. A good working relationship between therapist and client in SST can be formed very quickly, and when it does, it yields a good outcome (Simon et al., 2012). This framework can help explain why.

# 14

# From theory to practice I: Guidelines for good practice

## Abstract

*In this chapter, I consider four main theoretical SST principles and discuss how they lead to guidelines for good SST practice. The principles are:*

- *One session may be enough. Help the client get the most out of it, whether or not another one is needed*
- *The session is important, but not all important*
- *It is best to go slowly, be steady and be humble*
- *Genuine optimism about what clients are capable of*

*Many writers on SST have developed lists of the do's and don'ts of good practice in SST (e.g. Bloom, 1992; Dryden, 2017; Paul & van Ommeren, 2013 and Talmon, 1990). In this chapter, I consider guidelines for good practice but link them to the key theoretical principles as summarised above.*

## One session may be enough. Help the client get the most out of it, whether or not another one is needed

One of the critical theoretical assumptions of SST is what may be called 'the flexible power of the one'. By which is meant, that there is a lot that can be achieved if client and therapist 'roll up their sleeves' and deal with the client's issue and that this power can be harnessed if the therapist follows specific guidelines. However, all the work does not have to be done in this one session, and further sessions are possible.

This assumption spawns the following guidelines for good practice which will help the client get the most out of the session, whether or not it is the only one that the client has.

## Engage the client quickly through the work

The therapist utilising all the time that they have with the client is a central part of SST. Thus, the therapist gets down to work as quickly as possible. As discussed in the previous chapter, the bond between therapist and client is strengthened when this happens. Also, the client gets the sense that the therapist is keen to help, which results in the client joining the therapist in this endeavour.

## Be clear about why we are here

Therapist clarity aids the SST process in the sense that all concerned know why they are there and what their common task is. In this way, any client misconceptions about the purpose of the session can be identified, discussed and resolved.

## Be prudently active

The therapist needs to take an active role but one that also encourages the client to be active. Active collaboration is a feature of effective SST.

## Be focused and help the client stay focused

When the therapist creates a focus for the session, this should ideally be based on the client's view of their problem and what they want to achieve in relation to that problem.[1] Once created, the therapist helps the client stay focused.

## Develop a negotiated solution

In one sense, all SST is solution focused in the sense that the therapist strives with the client to find a solution that will deal with the problem and help goal attainment. Tentative solutions may be put forward by both and then discussed, culminating in the client selecting the one that has the most meaning for them and is most likely to work.

## Practise the solution in the session

Once a solution has been selected, the client is invited to practise this in the session, if feasible. This immediate practice helps the client to see what it feels like to implement the solution and what, if any, modifications may be necessary.

## Tie up loose ends and discuss possible future sessions

It is essential that the session is ended on a high note if possible, with the therapist answering any client questions and responding to any client doubts, reservations and objections. Part of a good closure concerns the situation regarding further sessions. The client needs to know what to do if they need further help in the near future or further down the line.

## The session is important, but not all important

One of the ironies of SST (and there are many) is that while there is much potential power to harness from the first (and perhaps only) session, the session is not all important in the change process. There is also much the client can gain from all that life has to offer and encouraging clients to develop such a mindset means that they will continue a process of change that started even before they had the session.

## Help the client to see that change may have already started

It often happens that when a person has made a decision to take steps to seek help, then they initiate a process of change that sometimes results in them cancelling any session they may have booked with a therapist. If the client does attend therapy, the SST therapist enquires to see what has changed since they decided to seek help and encourages the client to capitalise on any changes that they have made.

## External resources may be as helpful as internal strengths

The SST therapist knows that there is a wealth of external resources in the client's environment they can draw upon to help solve their problem. Orienting the client to this can be liberating for the client who comes to realise that only they can do it, but they do not have to do it alone.

## Extra-therapy events can help the client to change

A number of years ago a man booked a single session with me and the night before he went out for a meal with some friends. At that meal, he opened up to them about his problem and got a tremendously supportive response from them with several saying they too had also struggled with what he was struggling with. He found the evening profoundly therapeutic and only came to see me out of courtesy. I reinforced some of the things he had concluded from the night before, and he left. I had done very little. He did the real work the night before with his friends.

SST therapists are happy to hear such stories because they know that change can come from a myriad of sources and not just the single session.

## It is best to go slowly, be steady and be humble

You might think it strange that slowness, steadiness and humility underpin SST practice, Surely it should be: quickness, animation and supreme confidence?

## Take your time

When a single-session therapist knows what they are doing, they know that the best way to conduct the session is slowly. Working at a fast speed is often fuelled by anxiety, and an anxious SST therapist will not do an adequate job. It is surprising how much ground can be covered when an SST therapist works slowly and carefully, but in a focused manner with a client.

## One step forward may be enough to get change underway

Given SST's view of the change process as being something that probably started before the session and can continue after it, the SST therapist is happy if they have helped a client to take the first step because they know that if they encourage the client to use their strengths and capabilities, then they have helped them to take a step in the right direction. They then and can then take another step and another step etc. going forward.

**Be honest when you do not know.** Many therapists are frightened to say 'I do not know' to clients for fear of looking bad in the client's eyes. However, the SST therapist knows the value of humility and that actually most clients appreciate such honesty. Furthermore, the therapist's view is that their skills are more important than knowledge in facilitating change in SST and if they don't know something, they could always find out.

## Be genuinely optimistic about what clients are capable of

Without a genuinely optimistic outlook of what clients can achieve from SST, the therapist will think that facilitating client change in SST is down to them. This results in them putting themselves under pressure, and SST therapists do not work well under pressure.

## Identify the client's strengths and encourage them to use them

A defining feature of SST is the emphasis placed on client empowerment and client strengths. Helping clients to identify and reconnect with their strengths and then be asked to think how they might apply these strengths to their current concern is a common strategy in SST. Furthermore, they show the client that the therapist has faith in their capabilities and this helps them to feel more empowered.

## Identify helpful attempts to solve the current and other problems and encourage their use

While the client may still have the problem, it is possible that they have tried various things in the past to address it, some of which may have yielded some benefit. If so, the therapist can help them to distil the helpful ingredients and apply them anew to the problem, perhaps with some embellishments suggested by the therapist.

Also, the therapist can encourage the client to draw on what they did to solve other problems and use these helpful strategies to address their current concern. This can be seen as encouraging the client to get the most out of themself and in doing so to get the most out of the SST process.

## Encourage the client to take away learning from the session and apply it

In SST, the client is seen as capable of applying the negotiated solution to where it matters in their everyday life. However, they do need some encouragement to do so. In this regard, the therapist can suggest the use of action planning and mental rehearsal as useful ways of bridging the gap between practising the solution in the session and implementing it in the client's life.

## *Note*

1   This may not apply to solution-focused single-session therapists who
    tend to eschew working with problems.

# 15

## From theory to practice II: What to avoid[1]

### Abstract

*I would say that the efficient use of time is one of the key principles of single-session therapy. Here, the therapist is mindful that they may only have one session with the client, and as such, they need to use this knowledge to intervene accordingly. In the previous chapter, I outlined the types of interventions the SST therapist makes when they are using time efficiently. In my view, learning is enhanced when good practice is contrasted with bad practice so, in this chapter, I do two things. First, I review activities that therapists may implement when they do not have the efficient use of time at the forefront of their minds. This may be the case with therapists who work within generous time limits (e.g. 12–20 sessions) or who work with clients in an ongoing manner where the end of therapy is not specified. Please note that in listing these activities, I am advising SST therapists to refrain from their use as I make clear. Second, I review activities which stem from therapists being intimidated by the time limits inherent in SST.*

### When time is not at a premium

When therapists are not working under the felt limitations of time, they tend to engage in the following therapeutic activities. I want to stress, at the outset, that these activities may well have merit given the context of the time such therapists have with their clients. However, as we will see, they are counterproductive when applied to SST. In discussing each activity, I will give reasons for their use. Again, such reasons need to be considered within the context of freedom from the tight limitations of time present in SST.

## Taking an elaborate history

Taking an elaborate history is vital because it helps the therapist to understand the person within the rich context of their developing history. Each person is unique and is best understood when the following information is obtained:

- upbringing and relationships with parents, siblings and other family members
- schooling and educational and social development (e.g. relationships with peers)
- relationship and sexual history particularly with an emphasis on their problematic aspects
- occupational history and relationships with bosses and work colleagues
- hobbies and recreational activities
- history of psychological problems and especially any episodes of suicide attempts and self-harm
- problematic use of substances (e.g. alcohol and drugs)
- history of physical problems
- current evidence of risk of harm to self and others.

In taking a history, the therapist is looking for patterns that may relate to current problems.

**SST view: Don't take an elaborate history.** In the film *Ghost Town*, Ricky Gervais plays a cynical New York dentist who goes to A&E complaining of bowel problems. At intake, he is asked some questions about his history to which he replies 'irrelevant'. This is a good reminder for the SST therapist only to ask questions that are relevant to the client's concerns. The therapist does not have the time or the reason to take an elaborate history.

## Letting the client talk in an unfocused way

When clients come to therapy, they may experience for the first time an opportunity to talk about themselves in whichever way they choose, free from the constraints of other people's agendas. The therapist only has one agenda: to listen to the client and provide them with help in an unrushed environment. Additionally, coming to therapy may be the first time the client has had an opportunity to talk about themselves in a personal way. For both of these reasons, it is vital for the client to talk in their own way, at their own pace.

**SST view: Don't let the client talk in an unfocused, general way.** In general, left to their own devices, clients will talk about their concerns in a general way without focus, as noted above. Given that time is at a premium in SST, such general, unfocused talk will not help the client to get much out of the single session. Working with specificity and focus is what is needed in SST.

## Listening and responding from the client's frame of reference

As we have seen, it is important to give new clients an extended opportunity to talk in their own way at the beginning of therapy. The therapist's role here is to listen attentively and non-judgmentally and not impose a direction on the client. While the client is exploring themselves in this unfocused way, the therapist seeks to convey their understanding of the client from their frame of reference. The therapist does not impose time limits on themselves concerning how long they will stay in this mode of listening and responding, as they take the client's lead. When the client becomes more focused so will the therapist.

**SST view: Don't spend too much time in non-directive, listening mode.** While it is important for clients in SST to be heard, the SST therapist ensures they give their non-judgmental attention to the client while helping them to focus on their prime concern. They consequently do not spend too much time in a non-directive, listening mode.

## Assessing problems comprehensively

In therapy free from time pressure, the therapist has the time to do a thorough assessment of the problems that clients present for help. As it is not clear what may be relevant and what may not be relevant, the therapist errs on the side of caution and collects a lot of data even though they may not use much of this information later. From this perspective, it is better to have something and not use it than miss something that was crucial.

**SST view: Don't assess where not relevant.** Not all SST therapists engage in problem assessment, but those who do avoid assessing areas that may be useful to know about, but is unnecessary to the focus of SST. In my practice of SST, I usually spend much time in problem assessment mode. In particular, it is vital for me to know precisely what adversities my clients struggle with and how they inadvertently maintain their problem. However, this assessment is done in a focused way, with little, if any, unnecessary data gathering (Dryden, 2017, 2018a).

## Carrying out a case conceptualisation

Case conceptualisation involves the therapist and client working together to gain an overall picture of the factors that account for the development and maintenance of the client's problems and how they may be linked. Increasingly, in CBT the view is that it is best not to initiate treatment unless one has carried out such a conceptualisation as this would be like trying to get somewhere unfamiliar without a map. It may take two or three sessions to develop such a conceptualisation. Also, if an elaborate history has been taken, then we may be into the fifth or sixth session before intervention starts. This is not an issue in longer-term therapy as long as the client understands and agrees with the rationale for these activities.

**SST view: Don't carry out an elaborate case conceptualisation.** While carrying out a case conceptualisation may be a valuable exercise, there is no time in SST for the therapy dyad to engage in it and this is why I say that SST is assessment, not conceptualisation driven (Dryden, 2017). This poses a challenge for those CBT therapists who find it difficult to intervene without being informed by a case conceptualisation.

## When the SST therapist is intimidated by time

Some therapists are intimidated by the idea that they may have only one session to help the person. From my REBT perspective, my hunch is that either such therapist believes that they must use time effectively and that they must help the person within this timeframe or they cannot tolerate the limits inherent in SST. Such therapists are advised to develop a flexible attitude towards time and helping and learn to tolerate the limits, which will help them to see the advantages that there are in working within such limits (see Chapter 3 and the case of Rod Temperton).

When a therapist is intimidated by time they tend to:

### Rush and overload their client

The time-intimidated SST therapist has an idea of what they want to cover in a session and rushes through it rather than focus on one or two key points. They struggle with the SST view that 'less is more'. The result is that the client is feels rushed, uncomfortable and confused.

**SST antidote: Don't rush the client.** Just because time is at a premium in SST (Dryden, 2016), it does not follow that SST therapists rush their clients. In fact, those who do are generally ineffective. I often point to the example of Mesut Özil, the Arsenal footballer, who is very effective, but never seems to be in a rush. Good SST therapists take their time!

### Assume that their client knows what they (the therapist) are doing and why

Here the therapist thinks that they do not have the time to explain their interventions and the reasons for making them even if they pick up that their client may have doubts about them. Actually, given that the therapist is under time pressure, they probably won't even pick up that the client may have such doubts.

**SST antidote: Don't assume that the client knows what the therapist is doing or why they are doing it.** It is tempting for therapists to think that if clients give non-verbal signs that they understand that they know what their therapists are doing and the reasons for doing it, then they do, in fact, understand. Good SST therapists do not make this assumption and will err on the side of caution by explaining what they do and why they are doing it. Moreover, they think that they have the time to do it.

## Ask multiple questions

If the client pauses to think about their answer to a question, the time-intimidated SST therapist considers this as time wasted and asks another version of the question or a different question entirely.

**SST antidote: Don't ask multiple questions.** SST therapists tend to ask many questions, but show patience in doing so. They avoid asking clients multiple questions if answers are not quickly forthcoming. Good SST therapists give their clients time to think.

## Note

1   From an SST perspective, not necessarily from their own perspective!

# Part 2

# PRACTICE

# 16

# Overview: The process of SST

## Abstract

*In this chapter, I consider two perspectives on the process of single-session therapy. These will serve as an overview for the rest of the chapters in the practical part of this book. The first perspective is perhaps more relevant to where the therapist is working alone. Following Hoyt (2000), there are six phases of SST: i) decision; ii) preparation; iii) beginning; iv) middle; v) ending; and vi) follow-through and follow-up. I briefly discuss what tends to happen at each phase. The second perspective is perhaps more relevant to walk-in therapy and where there is a team approach. Following McElheran, Stewart, Soenen, Newman & MacLaurin (2014), there are five phases of SST: i) pre-session; ii) the session with a focus on the presenting issue; iii) an inter-session consultation; iv) delivery of the intervention; and v) post-session debriefing.*

## Perspective 1: Where the therapist is working alone

It is not unusual for therapists to take a process view of therapy (e.g. Garfield, 1995) and this perspective is most likely to be taken when therapy lasts for longer than a single session. However, Hoyt (2000) has brought a process perspective to SST, and I have drawn on his ideas in this chapter.

## The decision phase

In the decision phase, the person seeking help has contacted the therapist, and the two of them need to decide whether or not they both want to engage in SST and whether or not this way of working best meets the person's therapeutic needs. I discuss this issue in greater detail in the next chapter.

## The preparation phase

Hoyt et al. (2018b) distinguish between SST by appointment and SST by walk-in. In the former, the therapist has an opportunity to engage the person seeking help in a conversation designed to help them get the most out of the process. This conversation most often takes place over the telephone, but it can happen in any medium. I discuss this issue in Chapter 18.

## The beginning phase

After contracting (see Chapter 19), the beginning phase of SST is marked by the therapist enquiring of the client what problem they want to address and/or what goal they want to achieve from the session (see Chapters 20 and 21). If they mention a longer-term goal, the therapist still helps them to set a session goal, which is framed as a step towards the longer-term goal. By getting down to work straight away and demonstrating a keenness to help the client, the therapist establishes a good working alliance with the client (see Chapter 13).

## The middle phase

Once the therapist and client know what the client wants to achieve, they get down to the business of what Hoyt calls 'refocus and change'. This is the phase where SST therapists bring to the process the insights and skills offered by their own therapeutic orientations and use them within the context of empowering the client by drawing on and encouraging them to use their inner strengths, competencies, resiliency factors and helping them to see how they can utilise their external resources (see Chapter 24). This is what I have called the SST fusion between what the client brings to the process and what the therapist brings to the process (see Chapter 7). Thus, in the middle phase, the therapist may work with the client to consider implementing a variety of potential solutions (see Chapters 23 and 26). These include i) identifying exceptions to their problem occurring and helping the client capitalise on these; ii) looking for and utilising instances of the goal happening; iii) encouraging the client to do something different; and iv) looking at things from a different perspective. The creative SST therapist often invents tailor-made interventions on the spot that are impactful and encourage the client to develop creative solutions that address their problems and/or facilitate movement towards their goal (see Chapter 25).

Later in the middle phase, the therapist helps the client to select a solution that they think will be most helpful to them (see Chapter 26) and encourages them, if possible, to practise the solution in the session (see Chapter 27).

## The ending phase

In the ending phase, the therapist encourages the client to summarise what they have learned from the session and to make plans to implement this learning. The therapist answers any last-minute questions that the client may have and generally ties up loose ends (see Chapter 28). An agreement is made concerning whether future sessions are possible and, if they are, what the client has to do to access these.

## The follow-through and follow-up phase

From one perspective this is not a part of the SST since the person may not return, which is most likely, perhaps, in SST by walk-in. From another perspective, usually the client's, it is a part of the SST process especially when it is framed as 'One-at-a-Time'

Therapy where the client can have a series of single sessions. Hoyt (2000) makes the useful distinction between follow-through, which concerns matters of client continuation and return, and follow-up, which concerns gaining feedback from the client concerning outcome and service evaluation after therapy has finished (see Chapter 30).

## Perspective 2: Walk-in therapy and where therapists work in a team

In describing walk-in therapy at Eastside Family Centre in Calgary, Alberta, Canada, McElheran, Stewart, Soenen, Newman & MacLaurin (2014) describe a different process of an SST session. This process view differs from the one described above in that it describes an approach to walk-in therapy where the client is a family rather than an individual who are helped by a therapy team as opposed to a therapist working alone. This process perspective is consistent with the Milan family therapy model (e.g. Boscolo, Cecchin, Hoffman & Penn, 1987) and appears to describe a lot of SST work with families carried out by therapists who are supported by an observing team.[1]

### The pre-session

This involves a review of any forms filled out by the client and of any other information to hand (e.g. notes if there has been previous contact by the client). The team formulate tentative hypotheses as a possible guide for the session and for testing within the session.

### The first half of the session

Here the client discusses why they are seeking help, and the therapist helps them to focus and address the presenting issue.

## The inter-session consultation

The treating therapist calls for a break and consults with the therapy team about the issue that has been co-created by the client and therapist, and the whole team discusses and puts forward an intervention.

## The second half of the session

The therapist offers commendations to the client and delivers the intervention on behalf of the therapy team.

## The post-session debriefing

After the client leaves, the therapy team discuss whether or not the client got what they wanted from the session and a note is made to guide future work if the client returns.

While two different perspectives on the process of SST have been presented, I will mainly use the first one to structure the rest of the book although many issues discussed will be relevant to both perspectives.

### Note

1   I will refer here to 'client' and 'therapist' even though the client may be a family and there may be more than one person in the role of therapist.

# 17

# Making a decision about SST

## Abstract

*In this chapter, I consider the issue of helping a person decide whether or not SST will be helpful to them. In doing so, I use a help-seeking framework that outlines the roles that a person may occupy when contacting a therapist or therapy service.*

When a person approaches a therapist or a therapy service, they occupy one of three help-seeking roles. It is useful for the SST therapist and the person who takes such calls in a therapy agency to consider which role a person may occupy when deciding whether or not a person may benefit from SST. This tends only to apply to SST by appointment rather than SST by walk-in, where the therapist needs to deal with the person no matter which of the following roles they may occupy.

## Different help-seeking roles

There are a number of roles that a person may occupy with respect to help-seeking. I will consider this issue concerning my practice.

### The 'contemplator' role

When a person is in the 'contemplator'[1] role, they recognise that they have a problem and are thinking about what to do about it. If they have decided to think about seeking help, they have not made any direct approaches to potential helpers. Instead, they may have spoken to people about potential helpers or organisations where they can seek help.

### The 'enquirer' role

When a person is in the 'enquirer' role, they are making direct approaches to potential therapists or organisations offering therapeutic help. The 'enquiring' mindset is to find out more about therapeutic services directly and to discover what such services may cost. However, the person has not yet decided to seek help from any particular therapist.

### The 'applicant' role

When a person is in the 'applicant' role, they have decided that they want to seek help from a particular therapist and agency and can thus be seen to have applied for such help. However, they cannot yet be appropriately considered to be a client.

### The 'client' role

When a person is in the client role, they have agreed with the therapist what service they are going to receive. They understand the nature of that service together with its potential benefits and possible risks and have decided to give their informed consent. At the point when they have given such consent, then they can be said to become a client.

### The pathway

When a person contacts me, usually by phone or by email, they are directly contacting me as I have no secretarial or administrative support. I undertake to give an immediate response to anybody making contact with me. In the case where somebody has left me their number, I call them back to discover whether they are in the 'enquirer' role or the 'applicant' role.

## Responding to those in the 'enquirer' role

If a person is in the 'enquirer' role, I try to find out what questions they have to help them determine whether they wish to make an application to see me. This may result in my telling them what I charge or what services I offer in a general way.

## Responding to those in the 'applicant' role

If a person is in the 'applicant' role, they may know that I offer SST and are clear that this is the kind of help that they seek or they may not know about my SST service. If they are seeking SST, I ask them to tell me briefly why they think that this service may be particularly helpful to them and as they respond, I listen to see if I agree with them or not. If I do agree, I tell them about the way I tend to work with SST (see Dryden, 2017) and book a pre-session telephone contact with them the next day if possible. The purpose of this contact is to hear a little more about their issue and to gain information from them designed to help them get the most out of their single face-to-face session with me. This session is booked again very soon after the pre-session telephone contact if we have both decided that SST is the best option for the person. If I do not agree, I explain why and offer a different service. In my view, SST needs to be a mutually agreed way forward for the person.

With general applicants, my practice is to tell them about the range of services that I offer: SST, ongoing therapy, couples therapy and coaching, and then ask them which service would best meet their needs. If they nominate SST, I invite them to explain why and if I agree, I explain the way I work with SST (as above) and move to the next stage, which is to schedule a pre-session telephone contact. If I do not agree, I again explain why and offer a service that I think will better meet their needs. This may be with another practitioner or with me.

## *Note*

1   This is different from 'contemplation' in the 'stages of change' model where the person is contemplating whether or not they have a problem. (Prochaska, Norcross & DiClemente, 2006).

# 18

## Preparing for the session

### Abstract

*In this chapter, I consider the issue of how best the therapist and client can prepare for the face-to-face session so that the client can get the most from it. I cover both the context of such preparation and the content.*

As every gardener knows, it is vital to prepare the ground before planting seeds. If this is not done, then weeds in the unprepared ground may impair the growth of these seeds with the result that the gardener will not get as much from the ground as they would do if it was adequately prepared.

This analogy applies to SST as well. The first (and perhaps only) session has a lot of potential benefits to be gained by the client. However, for these benefits to be realised the therapist needs to work with the client to prepare for this session. Before I discuss the nature of this preparation, let me first review the contexts in which it can take place.

### Contexts for session preparation

Session preparation can take place in a number of contexts. Here I review some of the main contexts.

## Pre-session telephone contact

Often preparation for the session takes place over the telephone. The therapist and client agree to talk over the telephone, and the client is informed that the purpose of this conversation is for both parties to discuss how they might prepare so that the therapist helps the client to get the most out of the face-to-face session that is to follow.[1] It is important that this session is arranged to be held at a time where the client and therapist can give one another their full attention and where the client will not be interrupted or disturbed. I recommend that the client has a notebook to hand to make notes from the conversation and I do the same.

Different therapists have different ways of structuring the telephone conversation. My practice is to refer to a protocol when asking questions to get the information that I think will help me to best help the person (Dryden, 2017). However, it is equally useful for the client to ask me questions that, from their perspective, will help them to get the most out of the session.

## Pre-session questionnaire

Many agencies that offer SST have a pre-session questionnaire for the client to complete and submit before they attend the session. Such a questionnaire can be completed on a physical form or online. The key points here are that it is completed and submitted as close to the session as possible so that it reflects the client's current situation and that the therapist has an opportunity to read the form and digest the information. Table 18.1 presents the questions asked in one pre-session questionnaire.

In walk-in therapy clinics, the person can be asked to complete a brief pre-session questionnaire as there is generally a short wait before the person can be seen and this is an excellent way for the waiting time to be used.

**Table 18.1 Walk-in counselling clinic client questionnaire**

1. Have you received services from our agency in the past or have you ever contacted our 24-hour Crisis Line before?

2. Why have you come today?

3. If 1 is the worst and 10 is the best, how are things in your life today?

4. What would be the best thing that could happen in this meeting today?

5. What is the one problem that seems most important to work on now?

6. What is it like when this problem is around?

7. Are you currently at any risk of harm to yourself or to others? YES/NO

8. What would someone else like and respect most about you if they had a lot of time to get to know you?

9. For us to be most helpful is there anything you feel is important for us to know about your culture, ethnicity, religion, language, sexual orientation, gender identity/expression, mental or physical health, or other?

(Reach Out Centre for Kids, Ontario, 2017)

## At the beginning of the session

It is possible for such preparation to take place in the face-to-face session. Here the therapist says that they would like to get vital information from the client before the session gets underway so that they can help the person get the most out of it. Note that a distinction is being made here between a period before the session starts and the session itself. This is best done when the contact between therapist and client is longer than usual (e.g. 90 minutes as opposed to 60 minutes). Again the client is also invited to contribute to this process as an active partner.

### Content for session preparation

What does the therapist want to know when preparing for the session so that they can help the client get the most out of the session? While

SST therapists will differ on this issue, what follows is a range of topics that might be included in the content of the pre-session preparation contact with suggestions of how they might be used in the session.[2]

- What are the reasons you are seeking help now?
- Who else is involved?
- How quickly do you want to be helped?
- What would like to achieve by the end of the session?
- What previous attempts have you made to solve the problem and what was the outcome?
    - Utilise helpful attempts; discourage unhelpful attempts
- How have you solved similar problems in the past?
    - Suggest transferring successful strategies to the  problem
- What relevant *strengths* do you have that you can bring to the process of SST?
- What *character virtues* do you have that will help you get the most from our work together?
- What important *values* do you have that might underpin our work?
- How can I best help you when we have our face-to-face session?
- What *external resources* can you make use of that might be a benefit in therapy?
- What *music, literature and pieces of art* do you associate with effecting change*?*
- What *valuable lessons* has life taught you?
- What *principles of living* guide you?
- What *role models or influential figures* might encourage you to change in the way you want?

Again let me stress that I am not advocating that the SST therapists ask their clients all of these questions. Preferably, they are to be used as a resource to select from, as appropriate.

PRACTICE

## *Notes*

1 By face-to-face, I mean any setting in which the therapist and client can see one another. This includes therapy where the two people are physically in the same room, or over the internet via a platform such as Skype.

2 Also see Table 18.1 for an example of such content.

94

# 19

# Contracting

## Abstract

*Contracting involves the therapist and client agreeing to work with one another based on a mutual understanding of the service that is on offer. I show how therapists might describe different forms of SST so that the client can give their informed consent to proceed.*

## Introduction

When the therapist and client meet for the face-to-face session, it is vital for both to be clear about several important issues concerning their contract. In this chapter, I will just focus on the nature of the service on offer to clients and how a therapist might make this explicit. I will not discuss other more general matters such as an agency's policy on confidentiality and risk assessment and management.

Here I will outline several different types of SST services and how they can be made explicit so that the client can give their informed consent to proceed, which becomes their contract. I will not discuss whether the contract should be in writing or agreed verbally as this is a more general therapeutic issue and pertains to all forms of service provision, not just SST issues.

## *Only one session*

As I discussed in Chapter 1, there are some SST therapists who only offer one session and some therapists who offer more, but may be in a position to only offer one, for a variety of reasons. Typically, this has been discussed before the client comes to the session. For example, I recently went to India and a few weeks before I left, someone rang me to see if they could book six sessions with me as they were visiting London for six weeks. Unfortunately, our diaries clashed and I was only able to offer the person one session, which they accepted. At the beginning of the session, I reminded the client that we had only one session, but that we could Skype afterwards. However, she was unable to Skype or WhatsApp, so this was to be the only session we had apart from a follow-up to be arranged when she next was going to come to London.

When, for whatever reason, there is to be only one session, the therapist might say something like, "As I discussed on the phone, we are only able to meet for one session, and you said that you were OK with that, but I just want to check with you that this is still the case." If it is, the therapist can follow-up with, "OK, so let's join forces and see if we as a team can help you take away something that will make a difference to you".

## *Walk-in therapy*

Walk-in services offer people the opportunity to be seen promptly without an appointment. Some people use a walk-in service once, while others may use it several times and different services have different stances concerning future sessions being available. Some state that a person may walk-in again while others say that if a further session is needed, then an appointment must be made (Dryden, 2019a). The critical point here is that the therapist should make it clear to the client what the policy of the service is before proceeding. Here is an example of what a therapist in one walk-in service might say:

Before we start, I just want to make clear what the policy of this service is so that you can give the go ahead. Here, we offer one session and together we will focus on helping you with whatever you have come with. My wish is that we get the job done today, but if not and you want to return then that is possible, and you can walk back in again. Is that clear? Do you have any questions? Shall we proceed on that basis?

## One session with the possibility of more

The current prevailing view in the SST community is that one session may be sufficient, but more sessions are available if needed. For example, a therapist may say something like, "We have agreed to meet today, and if we both really focus we can help you to head in a direction that is right for you, and if so, you may decide at the end that this is all that is needed. If not, further help is available. Shall we move forward on that basis?"

## One-at-a-Time (OAAT) Therapy

OAAT Therapy is a therapy in which the person has one session at a time. Here the therapist says something like:

In this clinic, we offer one session at a time. So today, we will see if we can team up to address your problem to your satisfaction. Then I will ask you to go away and reflect on what you have learned, digest it and then put it into practice. Then, after you have let things settle, if you decide that you need another session, please get back in touch, and you can book another session. If I have not helped you to your satisfaction today, then you can book another session with me or with one of my colleagues. How does that sound to you?

## Unique features

If there are any features that are unique to the therapist's practice of SST, then the therapist should make them clear at the outset and seek the client's agreement. For example, in my own practice of SST, I ask for permission to record the session. I state that part of the SST package that I offer involves me sending the client a digital voice recording of the session and a written transcript of the recording for the client's later review. I make clear that while these are primarily for the benefit of the client, they also help me to reflect on my work and improve my service delivery (Dryden, 2017).

# 20

# Getting started

## Abstract

*In this chapter, I consider different ways of beginning the single session once contracting has been done. Getting started is different if there has been a pre-session contact between therapist and client than if there has been no such contact, as will be shown.*

After contracting has been done, the therapist and client are ready to begin the session. How the therapist begins the session depends, in part, on whether or not there has been any pre-session contact between them. In this chapter, I will consider both situations.

## Getting started when there has been pre-session contact

Pre-session contact between therapist and client may vary in length.[1] This contact may be very brief lasting from 5–10 minutes to establish that the person has expectations that are consistent with SST, where one session is available with the possibility of more. Alternatively, the contact may be much longer and oriented not only to confirm that the client's expectations are consistent with SST (as mentioned above) but also to help both parties prepare for the session so that the chances that the client will derive benefit from the session are increased.

Quite often at the end of the pre-session contact, the therapist might suggest that the client engages in a task between the pre-session contact and the face-to-face session. This is to build a bridge between the two contacts and either initiate a process of change or carry on such a process that has already been initiated by the client before they come to the session. Two such suggestions that SST therapists typically make are what can be termed 'noticing' and 'doing'.

## When the therapist has suggested a 'noticing' task

Talmon (1990: 19) gives one such example: "Between now and our first session, I want you to notice the things that happen to you that you would like to keep happening to you in the future. In this way, you will help me to find out more about your goal and what you are up to". At the beginning of the face-to-face session, the therapist might ask, "What changes have you noticed since we spoke on the phone?" If the client reports a change, then the therapist could ask:

- "What did you do to bring about that change?"
- "What effect is that change having?"
- "If we had not spoken and made this change by the end of this session, how would you feel about making the change?"

The client's responses suggest a way forward for the therapist regarding creating a possible focus for the session.

## When the therapist has suggested a behavioural task

Sometimes during the pre-session contact, what the client is talking about lends itself to a suggestion by the therapist for the client to do something between that contact and the face-to-face session. For example, Harry spoke about being anxious about the views of people older than him. Currently, he was anxious about his parents-in-law disapproving of him for wanting to move his family to a different part of the country. I asked him if he knew the viewpoint of his in-laws on this point? He said 'no', so I suggested that he do so before

**Figure 21.1** The process relating to the client's problem, goal and solution in SST

---

Problem ----→ Set Goal ----→ Negotiate and Implement Solution ----→
   Work Towards Goal

---

we had the face-to-face session with the promise that I would help him deal with his feelings should they show disapproval. When we met for the face-to-face session, I began by asking what happened when he told his in-laws of his plans:

*Windy:* How did the discussion with your in-laws go?

*Harry:* Much better than I thought.

*Windy:* What happened?

*Harry:* Well, I told them, and I was right. They did not like it. But as we were talking, I realised that I did not mind about this as much as I thought I would. I also surprised myself that I stood up for myself and made the point that I would look after their daughter and that seemed to reassure them a bit. We left on better terms than I thought.

*Windy:* What did you do to bring about this change?

*Harry:* Well you asked me to do it, but the main thing was that I decided to do it. When I made that decision, I noticed it calmed me down.

*Windy:* So deciding to take action is a good way to tackle anxiety.

*Harry:* Yes.

*Windy:* What else did you do to bring about change?

*Harry:* I think standing up for myself was useful.

*Windy:* So taking a decision to act and standing up for yourself were key ingredients in this situation. Let's keep these at the forefront of our minds as we talk in the session. OK?

*Harry:* OK.

*Windy:* Can I share something with you?

*Harry:* Sure

*Windy:* What struck me from what you said was that you spoke to them as an equal. I wonder what you think about that?

*Harry:* [pause] …Wow! That's spot on. With all these older people, I don't see myself as their equal.

*Windy:* So that sounds like something we really need to focus on and link it to what you took from the experience. Does that make sense?

*Harry:* Yes, it does.

This is a clear example of how in SST much can be gained from a simple suggestion and how the therapist uses the client's experience of the task to begin the session and almost immediately focus on a central theme. It also shows the importance of the therapist's expertise in sharing an observation that the client missed when he was reflecting on his own experience.

### When the therapist has provided an email summary of the pre-session contact for the client

Sometimes, in my practice of Single-Session Integrated Cognitive Behaviour Therapy (Dryden, 2017), it helps me to reflect in writing on the complexities of a pre-session telephone contact. When I know I am going to do this, at the end of the contact I ask the client if they would find it useful to receive a copy of my written reflections by email. Almost always the client says yes, in which case I write to the client. At the end of the email, I usually ask the client to reflect on its contents and focus on anything that resonates with them and to take any action based on that resonance if it makes sense to do that.

At the beginning of the face-to-face session, I refer to the email in one of the following ways:

- "What did you make of the email summary that I sent you?"
- "Did anything that I wrote resonate with you?" If so, I ask "What resonated with you?"
- "Did you try out anything based on what resonated with you?"

- "Has anything changed concerning your problem after reading the email summary? If so, what did you do to bring about that change?"

The client's responses again suggest a way forward for the therapist regarding creating a possible focus for the session.

## Getting started when there has been no pre-session contact

When there has been no prior contact between the therapist and client before the session, as in walk-in SST, the therapist can begin the session in the following ways:

### Problem and solution-focused SST

When the therapist adopts a problem and solution-focused approach, they might begin by asking the client:

- "What problem do you have?"
- "If we were only going to meet once, what problem would you want to focus on solving at this point?" (Haley, 1989)

### Solution-focused SST

When taking a solution-focused approach, the therapist might ask:

- "If you were to go home today and think that the session was worthwhile, what would have happened?"
- "What are you willing to change today?" (Goulding & Goulding, 1979)
- "What are your best hopes for today's meeting?" (Iveson, George & Ratner, 2014)

In both cases, the client's answers allow the therapist to pick up the baton and use the responses to begin the process of change.

## *Note*

1 I will assume here that such contact is by telephone or by Skype, but that it is not face-to-face with the therapist and client meeting in the same room.

# 21

# Working with problems and goals

## Abstract

*SST therapists differ concerning what issues they attend to during the single session. Some attend to problems, goals and solutions, while others attend to goals and solutions. It is unlikely that there are too many SST therapists working with clients' problems alone without reference to goals and solutions. In this chapter, I consider how SST therapists can work with problems and goals and will consider how they work with solutions in Chapter 26.*

When a client comes to therapy, it is usually because they are in some kind of problematic state and are looking for help with that state. This state is typically called a 'problem'. What the client hopes to achieve from therapy is to arrive at or return to a non-problematic state. This state is typically called a 'goal'. A 'solution' is a means of addressing the problem that moves the person closer to their goal. In my training workshops, I use a simple diagram to illustrate this, which I reproduce in Figure 21.1. This figure shows that the therapist begins by focusing on the problem, then helps the client to set a goal which influences the negotiation of a solution. The client then implements the negotiated solution which takes them closer towards their goal.

In this chapter, I will discuss how SST therapists work with problems and goals since these are therapists' tasks that are closer to the beginning of the session. Since working with solutions comes later, I will consider them later in this book (see Chapter 24).

Before I start, I want to make the point that some SST therapists tend only to work with goals and solutions (e.g. solution-focused therapists). Such therapists tend to see working with problems as focusing on the negative and on what is wrong with the client. By working with goals and solutions, such therapists consider that they are working with the realistically positive and focusing on what is right with the client. Other SST therapists argue that as clients expect to talk about their problems, a certain amount of focused time can usefully be spent in SST on doing so since this can reveal what the client has a problem with and how they unwittingly maintain the problem. Of course, these SST therapists also work with goals and solutions.

## Working with the problem

When working with the client's problem, it is vital that the therapist does this in a way that conveys to the client that the problem is solvable. There are two components of working with a problem: a) identifying the problem and b) assessing its main features.

### Identifying the problem

A client may come to SST with a number of problems. When this is the case, as there is probably only time for therapist and client to deal with one, the therapist needs to help the client to select one. Here are a number of questions that the therapist can ask when identifying the client's problem for SST:

- "What problem do you want to solve today?"
- "Imagine that when you get home today, we have successfully worked together to solve one of your problems. What problem would you want us to have solved?"
- "Of these problems, which one is it most important for you to solve?"[1]
- "If we tackled one of your problems successfully today, which one would give you the sense that you have made a significant step forward?"

## Assessing the problem

Once the client has identified a problem to focus on, the next stage is for the therapist to help the client to assess the problem. Such an assessment is going to depend, in part, on the professional constructs that the therapist uses to make sense of such problems, and in part on the client's view of this issue.

In my single-session practice, I am keen to understand the main adversity that features in the client's problem, their main problematic emotion, unconstructive behaviour and highly distorted thinking. Also, I am interested to learn about the contribution that any significant others make to the problem.

## Negotiating a goal

Usually, the client's goal relates to their problem. However, as solution-focused therapists (e.g. Ratner, George & Iveson, 2012) note, a therapist can negotiate goals with the client without reference to the client's problem.

### Negotiating a goal concerning the client's problem

When the SST therapist is negotiating a goal with a client concerning that person's problem, my view is that the achievement of the goal needs to be realistic. Thus, if the client's problem is anxiety about being judged negatively by others in a social situation and the client nominates a goal which involves being confident in such social situations, such a goal is realistic if it rests on the person first dealing productively with negative judgments from others. If it is not, and the client wants to bypass dealing with such judgments, then in my view this is unrealistic as it is difficult to develop social confidence when one is anxious about being negatively judged by others. Here, the therapist's task is to help the client to understand this and to nominate 'dealing productively with adverse social judgment' as their goal for SST, which is then spelt out. This example points to the distinction between 'dealing with problem' goals and 'enhancing development' goals. A good rule is: negotiate and help the client pursue the former before you accept and help them to pursue the latter (Dryden, 2018b).

Here, the therapist might ask:

- "What goal would you like to achieve concerning your problem?" This is known as an *outcome* goal and may not be able to be achieved in SST.
- When a client sets an outcome goal, the SST therapist might ask, "If I helped you today to take one step that would give you a sense that you were on the way to achieving your goal, what would that step be?" This can be seen as a *process* goal and is a more constructive goal for SST than an outcome goal. It can also be seen as a *session* goal since the client is being asked to nominate a goal to be achieved by the end of the session.
- Session goals are probably the favoured goal of SST therapists.

Negotiating a goal without reference to the client's problem. Here, given that the therapist is seeking to negotiate a goal without reference to the client's problem, goal-setting questions can be used to kick-off the SST process as we have seen in the previous chapter. For example, I mentioned in that chapter the question suggested by Iveson, George & Ratner, (2014), "What are your best hopes for today's meeting?", which can be seen as a session goal. Another session goal has been suggested by Talmon (1993: 40)

- "What would you like to accomplish today?"

## SMART goals

Whether goals are negotiated concerning problems or not, it is a good idea if they are 'SMART'. This is an acronym that stands for:

**'S' = Specific.** Specific goals should be clear enough to help the client see for what they are aiming.

**'M' = Motivating.** While 'M' usually stands for 'measurable', my view is that 'motivating' is more useful for SST, particularly if it makes clear what the reasons are for change.

**'A' = Achievable.** Only achievable goals have a place in SST.

**'R' = Relevant.** The goal needs to be relevant to the client's life if they are to work to achieve it.

**'T' = Time-bound.** It is important that the goal can be achieved in a specified period of time. What is most important is that if the goal can't be achieved by the end of the session, then the client can see where they are heading and can use the strengths to get there after therapy has ended.

### Note

1   When the client has mentioned more than one.

# 22

# Creating and maintaining a session focus

## Abstract

*In this chapter, I point out that the therapist needs to create a focus related to the client's problem, goal and solution or related just to the goal and solution. I discuss the natural human tendency to wander away from a focus, especially in conversations, and argue that polite, respectful interruption is what the therapist should do if the client departs from the agreed session focus. I then consider why therapists may have a problem with interrupting their clients and what they need to do about it. I conclude by considering what to do if the client departs from an agreed focus by not answering the therapist's key questions.*

Once the client and therapist have begun work, their next task is to create a focus for the session. This focus may have a number of components, which it is the therapist's task to connect. Thus, the dyad's focus may comprise a problem, a goal and a solution, as mentioned in the previous chapter or merely a goal and a solution.

As I made clear in Chapter 13 on the working alliance, it is crucial for the therapist and client to agree on their view of the problem, the client's goals and what constitutes an acceptable solution. Consequently, it is useful for the therapist to check periodically that the focus is still an agreed one. It may need to be modified as the session unfolds, but if it is modified too often, this is not a good sign.

## The natural human tendency to wander and become distracted

Most human beings find it difficult to stay focused on a task even if the task and the goal that it leads to are meaningful to them. Our minds wander, and it is a fundamental rule of meditation that when a person is focusing on their mantra, other thoughts will come into their mind. The person is advised to accept the presence of these thoughts and then go back to focusing on their mantra.

This process also happens in conversation. In social communication, people range over a number of topics with one topic stimulating another as two people enjoy each other's company. Even in a purposeful conversation, where the goal is to discuss one topic and come to a conclusion, people still get distracted and wander away from the focus. SST is one such purposive conversation and therefore given that some clients will find it easier to stay focused than others, the therapist needs to be able to help those who find it difficult to create and maintain the focus.

Clients wander away from the agreed session focus in two ways. First, they provide too much information for the purposes of SST about the contexts in which their problem occurred, and second, they move away from the specific to the general when it is crucial for them to focus on the specific. In the first situation, the person needs to be helped to provide only the information that will help the dyad to address and solve the problem together. In the second situation, the client needs to be brought back to the specific context. This is primarily done in two ways. First, the therapist checks with the client if the two are still on track and second, the therapist needs to interrupt the client but do so politely and respectfully.

## Polite, respectful interruption

There are a number of issues that need to be addressed concerning interrupting clients, a task with which many therapists struggle.

## Provide a rationale for interrupting the client

One way of making it easier to interrupt the client is to provide them with a rationale for doing so. I usually say something like:

> To get the most from sessions like this, it is important that the therapist and client both stay focused on the client's goal. Some people find it hard to stay focused, and without realising it, they wander from the agreed topic at hand. In this case, their therapist needs to interrupt them tactfully to help them to get back on track.

## Ask for and obtain the client's permission to interrupt

Once the rationale has been provided, it is crucial for the therapist to ask the client for their permission for the therapist to interrupt them. Thus: "If that happens with us, may I have your permission to interrupt you and bring you back to the focus?" Clients who have a problem with staying focused generally recognise this and are relieved when the therapist offers to interrupt them and thus readily give their permission.

## When the therapist has a problem with interrupting clients

The difficulties therapists have with interrupting their clients tend to be twofold. First, many therapists think that it is essential to facilitate the client's self-exploration and that to interrupt their 'flow' is counterproductive even when the clients wander from issue to issue. This viewpoint is unhelpful in SST where the focus is on one issue rather than allowing the client to take the lead in opening the conversation up in a broader way.

Second, some therapists think that interrupting clients is rude. My response is that it can be rude to do so if the therapist does it rudely. However, if the therapist does it tactfully after giving the client a rationale and gaining their permission, then this does not constitute rude practice. It constitutes good practice in SST.

### Ensure that the client answers important questions or change tack

If the SST therapist asks the client a vital question within the created session focus, and the client does not answer the question, then the therapist needs to bring this to the client's attention and invite the client to give an answer. If the client continues not to answer the question, the therapist needs to inquire about the reason. The client's response needs to be considered within the SST time constraints and the therapist needs to makes a judgment call concerning whether or not to proceed with the question given these constraints. If a different tack can be taken to help the client find a solution, then it should be taken. Flexibility is key here as elsewhere in the SST process.

# 23

## Doing the work

### Abstract

*In this chapter, I discuss what SST therapists tend to do in the middle phase of the process which, as Hoyt (2000) notes, concerns refocus and change. I frame my discussion by showing what work therapists from the three major single-session traditions tend to do in this phase.*

What the therapist and client do, having created a session focus, is going to depend, in large part, on the SST therapist's view of how best to facilitate client change in the session. As I discussed in Chapter 5, there is no one SST approach. Instead, it is a mindset that the therapist brings to the process, and this mindset can be applied by therapists guided by a variety of therapeutic ideas and orientations. The common thread is that the therapist draws upon a range of client variables and encourages the client to use them while searching for a solution to solve their problem and achieve their goal or to take a key first step in that process, which they can continue on their own after the session. The diverse thread is, as I have said, that therapists bring a plethora of different ways of doing this. This is why I have called this chapter, 'Doing the work', to indicate such diversity.

### Doing the work: Three SST traditions

A therapeutic tradition is comprised of a number of specific therapeutic approaches that subscribe to a coherent set of ideas that influence practice. These approaches may have differences that may be barely observable to the outsider, but may be very important to the insider.[1] Elsewhere, I have used the terms 'constructive', 'active-directive' and 'pluralistic' as labels to describe the three major therapeutic traditions (Dryden, 2019a). In this chapter, I will give a flavour of how SST therapists from these three traditions do the work in the middle phase of the single session.

## Doing the work: The 'constructive' tradition

Hoyt et al. (2018a: 14) state that approaches within the constructive SST tradition are "non-pathologising, solution-focused, collaborative or narrative" in nature. Therapists from this tradition use their expertise to help clients to utilise their own, often overlooked or disregarded, expertise in discovering and implementing solutions to their problems. What such therapists tend not to do is focus on problems or offer the client a perspective on their problems and how to address them or on how to best choose their solutions and/or reach their goals. Therapists from this tradition are decidedly client-centred (Dryden, 2019a). Here is a sample of how constructive therapists tend to do the work in the middle phase of SST.

**Identifying exceptions.** Here, the therapist encourages the client to look for exceptions to the problem and focuses their attention on what they did to make the problem a 'non-problem'. Once such client-enacted strategies have been identified, the therapist works with the client to enable them to initiate and develop them (see Ratner et al., 2012).

**Identifying instances of the goal already happening.** As can be seen from the above, identifying exceptions does involve keeping the problem in the frame. Partly for this reason, practitioners of solution-focused therapy (SFT) moved away from this method to one that is more in keeping with the philosophy of SFT. This involves encouraging the client to identify instances when the person reached their goal. Once identified, the therapist helps the client to identify what it was that they did to achieve their goal, and once found the therapist encourages the client, as above, to use such strategies in the future.

**Identifying and transferring overlooked helpful strategies from other areas.** I once worked with a client (not in SST) who had a problem with criticism. I helped him to deal with his anxiety of being criticised by his boss in one session and in the next session he presented with anxiety about being criticised by his mother-in-law. When I asked him if he had put into practice what he had learned from our successful discussion about how to deal with his anxiety about his boss's criticism, since the factors were almost identical, he replied, "No, I didn't. It did not occur to me. If I knew I could do it then I would have done so". This taught me an excellent lesson. Left to their own devices, many clients are not good at self-generated transfer of learning from one context to another. Such generalisation needs to be built into the therapy process. This is what constructive therapists do. They search for strategies that clients have used to solve other problems and help them to see which of these strategies they could use to achieve their problem-related goal.

## Doing the work: The 'active-directive' tradition

In my view, therapists from an 'active-directive' tradition in SST differ from therapists in the 'constructive' tradition in that they are more likely to work with problems than their constructive colleagues and they bring to the process their views about how people develop and maintain problems and how they can address these problems effectively. However, in the spirit of collaboration and with due regard to the working alliance (see Chapter 13), such therapists do two things that I will discuss more fully in the section on the pluralistic tradition. First, they ask their clients for permission to give their views about the problem and how it may be addressed. Second, they invite the use of a range of client factors.

Hoyt et al. (2018a) give the following examples of active-directive approaches to SST: REBT/CBT, redecision/Gestalt, psychodynamic, and some forms of strategic therapy. In my view, there are many more differences in the content of ideas among active-directive approaches than there are among constructive approaches. Given this, let me outline what I tend to do in the middle phase of the single session as a representative of REBT/CBT within the active-directive tradition (see Dryden, 2017; 2018a).

**My practice: Problem assessment.** When the client and I agree which problem we are going to focus on, I will assess the problem using the 'ABC' framework of REBT, which I will only present if I have the client's permission to do so. I stress that this is one way of making sense of their problem, not the only way, and I am interested in their view about this and their own understanding of the factors involved in the problem and its maintenance. In working with the problem, I will ask the client for an example of it. This can be recent, vivid, typical or anticipated. I find it particularly useful to work with an anticipated example of the problem since it is easier for a client to apply learning to the same situation that we have chosen to work with (i.e. anticipated) than it is to take what they have learned from an assessment of a past example and apply it to an anticipated example. I will offer this rationale to the client. However, ultimately, I will go along with the client's choice on this matter.

In the 'ABC' framework, 'A' stands for the main _A_dversity that features in the client's problem, 'B' stands for the _B_asic rigid and extreme attitudes that the person holds towards the adversity and 'C' stands for the emotional, behavioural and cognitive _C_onsequences of holding the basic attitudes. I usually assess them in the order 'C', 'A', 'B'. Since the work goes much better when I have identified the client's adversity correctly, I often spend quite a bit of time identifying 'A' precisely (as shown in Dryden. 2018a).

**Setting adversity-related goals.** While I may have asked for the client's goal for the session earlier on in the session, it is vital for me to ask them for their goal in handling the adversity once I have discovered it. I would describe my practice of SST as adversity focused in that if I can help the person deal effectively with the identified adversity, or to take a significant step towards doing so, then I think that I have achieved my goal as an SST therapist.

**My practice: Helping people to begin the attitude change process.** I do not expect my client to have changed their attitude at the end of the first, and perhaps the only, session that they have with me. However, I can help them to take the first step towards it, and it is surprising how much long-term benefit people have derived from doing so (see Dryden, 2018a). There are a number of ways of facilitating attitude change in SST, and I refer the reader to Dryden (2017) and Dryden (2018a).

I will return to other aspects of my single-session practice in several of the following chapters.

## Doing the work: The 'pluralistic' tradition[2]

The above distinction between constructive and active-directive approaches is rather black and white, and the reality is probably less clear-cut. Thus, while I would probably place myself more in the 'active-directive' camp than in the 'constructive' camp, I do two things that might be more closely allied with 'constructive' practice in SST. First, I ask my clients if they would be interested in my view of their problem and how we might address it and only proceed when they agree to do so. In doing so, I would *also* seek their views on these two points and would incorporate these views into our joint work. Second, I would *also* actively identify and use the client factors that I identified in the pre-session contact that were relevant to the problem that my client and I were working on. So, while I would self-identify as an active-directive SST therapist, I am also influenced and guided by 'constructive' SST principles.

Moshe Talmon who, I would say, is more in the constructive SST camp than the active-directive camp, has given good examples of the pluralistic nature of his SST practice (Talmon, 2018: 153). Thus, in working with clients, he may at different times in the same session:

- validate a patient's story via empathic listening and challenge the problematic elements in the same storyline
- increase a sense of hope or a realistic sense of optimism, and help a person to accept certain parts of the harsh reality

- offer neutral (and at times passive, silent) listening in one part of a session, and in another part, present active, focused questions
- be non-directive at one point of the session, and at other times give prescriptive-like directions.

As the field of SST matures, I hope that therapists in the constructive and active-directive traditions will learn to appreciate and incorporate each other's strengths into their work in the same way as they identify and incorporate their clients' strengths. When this happens, perhaps a pluralistic practice will be predominant in the field of SST.

## *Notes*

1   As an example of this, see Gonzalez, Estrada & O'Hanlon (2011) on the differences between solution-focused therapy and solution-oriented therapy. Partly to distinguish itself from solution-focused therapy, O'Hanlon changed the name of solution-oriented therapy to possibility therapy.

2   The following are several pluralistic principles that are relevant to SST (taken from Dryden, 2019a, pp. 114–115).

- There is no one absolute right way of understanding clients' problems and solutions – different viewpoints are useful for different clients.
- There is no one absolute right way of practising SST – different clients need different things, and therefore SST therapists need to have a broad practice repertoire.
- Disputes and disagreements in the SST field may, in part, be able to be resolved by taking a 'both-and' perspective, rather than an 'either/or' one.
- It is important that SST therapists respect each other's work and recognise the value that it can have.
- SST therapists should ideally acknowledge and celebrate clients' diversity and uniqueness.
- Clients should ideally be involved fully throughout the SST process.

- Clients should ideally be understood in terms of their strengths and resources as well as their areas of struggle.
- SST therapists should ideally have an openness to multiple sources of knowledge on how to practise SST: including research, personal experience, and theory.
- It is important that SST therapists take a critical perspective on their own theory and practice: being willing to look at their own investment in a particular position and having the ability to stand back from it.

# 24

# Utilising client variables

## *Abstract*

*In this chapter, I focus on how SST therapists use client variables in the session in the service of the client's change process. I give examples showing the questions that a therapist can ask when using a client's strengths, their previous attempts to solve the problem and their role models in dealing with their problem and/or in the service of their goal.*

Single-session work is in large part based on the principle of client empowerment. The view is that the client has lost their way in life or has got stuck and has also lost touch with the strong and resilient parts of themselves. The therapist's primary task is to help the client to reconnect with those constructive parts of self and to see that they can be applied to help achieve their goal or to get unstuck. As I discussed in Chapter 18, if SST is by appointment, the therapist has an opportunity to have a conversation with the client designed to help them both work together so that the client gets the most from the session. If SST is by walk-in, however, the therapist needs to identify growthful client variables as the single session unfolds, 'on the hoof', as it were.

In Chapter 7, I considered what these client variables might be, and these are listed below as an aide-memoire so that readers can refer to it in this chapter.

**Important client variables in SST:**
Internal strengths
Values

Previous attempts to solve the problem
Successful attempts to deal with other problems
Helping others
Being helped by others
Role models
Guiding principles
External resources

Here are some examples of how to use client variables in SST.

## Using internal strengths

- "Which of the strengths that you listed when we spoke over the phone might help you to speak up when your boss tries to take advantage of you?"

  *If a client cannot remember their nominated strengths then the therapist can prompt as follows:*

- "You mentioned that persistence and the ability to understand people from their point of view are two of your main strengths. Would either or both of these help you to speak up to your boss?"

- "I made a note of the strengths that you mentioned when we spoke over the phone. Here is the list. Which of these strengths would help you to stand up to your boss?"

  *When the client nominates a particular strength, the therapist could ask questions such as:*

- "So, understanding people from their point of view is the strength that will help you the most to speak up to your boss if he tries to take advantage of you. How will you use that strength in the situation?"

  *It is useful to help clients take the generality of a particular strength and help them to specify how they would use it in a concrete situation.*

## *Using previous attempts to solve the problem*

Here is a dialogue between myself as therapist and a client that shows how a therapist can use the client's previous attempts to solve the problem to shape a better solution. Here the client is struggling with social anxiety when out on dates.

> *Windy:* So you mentioned a few things that you tried in the past that weren't helpful to you, like having a list of prepared topics to talk about and asking about hobbies. Why do you think that these were not helpful to you?
>
> *Jean:* Well they just came over as very trite.
>
> *Windy:* And you mentioned asking open-ended questions about what the other person was really interested in was the one thing you tried that was helpful. What was helpful about that?
>
> *Jane:* Well initially, it took the focus off of me, but as the person started talking and I showed genuine interest, he seemed to light up, and then he asked me about my interests, and we had a good conversation.
>
> *Windy:* So, what was the difference between the two strategies?
>
> *Jane:* The first was something I wasn't really interested in, but the second I was.
>
> *Windy:* So, how can you use this insight to help you deal with your fear of dating?
>
> *Jane:* To be genuinely interested in the other person.
>
> *Windy:* And how can you do that?
>
> *Jane:* By inviting them to talk about something that they are really into.

Note that in this segment, my interventions were mainly open-ended. I first asked the person to describe what they had tried that had not been helpful to them and then to describe what they had tried that had been helpful. Then I asked them what was different between the two strategies rather than offer my interpretation, which

I would have done if my open-ended approach did not bear fruit. I then invited them to think of how they could put their self-derived insight into practice.

## Using nominated role models

Here is another dialogue that I had with a client where I used one of the client's role models to good effect. The client could not think of having had any success with past attempts to solve their problem, which was feeling guilty about saying no to his mother when she made unreasonable requests of him.

> *Windy:* So, nothing that you have tried before has been helpful, even a little?
>
> *Jerry:* Not really. Alcohol helps in the short term, but I really don't want to go down that route.
>
> *Windy:* I get that. Do you recall in our telephone conversation to get the most out of this session, I asked you who your role models are?
>
> *Jerry:* Yes, I do. I mentioned three, I believe.
>
> *Windy:* Which of the three people you mentioned would have been able to solve the problem after grappling with it?
>
> *[Notice that I introduce the idea of solving the problem after grappling with it. I find that the most influential role models are those who struggle with and then overcome a problem. There needs to be a foundation of realism here]*
>
> *Jerry:* My cousin, Raphael.
>
> *Windy:* What makes you say that?
>
> *Jerry:* Well, he has had similar problems with his mother but has managed to say 'no'.
>
> *Windy:* How do think he managed that?
>
> *Jerry:* Well, knowing him, he would say 'no' to his mother and explain why. If she made unreasonable requests of him, I would see him roll his eyes to himself, but reiterate why he was not going to do what she requested.

*Windy:* What would he do or think not to feel guilty?

*Jerry:* I think he would remind himself that he is a good son and that if his mother was upset, then that was unfortunate, but it wasn't going to stop him from standing his ground.

*Windy:* OK. What can you learn from him?

*Jerry:* That if I am clear and kind... because Raphael is kind, I will know in my own mind that I am a good son and when my mother implies or tells me that I am not, I can see her behaviour for what it really is, an attempt to control me.

*Windy:* Can you imagine putting that perspective into practice?

*Jerry:* I think so.

[I then went on to encourage Jerry to practise this solution with me in the session (see Chapter 27).]

# 25

# Making an impact

### Abstract

*In this chapter, I show how to increase the impact that a session may have on a client in SST. However, first, I discuss several 'red flags' where the therapist needs to tread carefully when considering increasing the impact of their SST work.*

There are a number of principles in SST as I have made clear in this book. These can be expressed in pithy phrases such as:

- *'More haste, less speed'*, which sums up the idea that when an SST therapist rushes, they often make less progress than if they work at a steady pace.
- *'Sooner is better'*, which sums up the idea that when clients are seen quickly with a single session, they often do better than if they are placed on a lengthy waiting list for more sessions.
- *'More is less'*, which sums up the recognition that when the SST therapist tries to cover much ground in a session and wants the client to take away a lot, then this is frequently less effective than if they take away one meaningful point that they can implement immediately.

I maintain that such pithy phrases make the principles more memorable and thus have more impact on trainee SST therapists than if the more wordy versions of the principles were used. This is the main point of this chapter. If the therapist increases the impact of the single session, then the client is more likely to benefit from the session than if it lacked impact.

### First, a few red flags

I think that I can make this chapter more impactful if I first spell out a few words of warning.

### Less is more

It is crucial that the client is not overloaded with the therapist's smart 'impactful' interventions. If the client can take away one impactful point that has meaning for them, then this is better than several points of impact, most of which would soon be forgotten, probably including the one that had the most impact on them.

### Don't emotionally overstimulate a client

A good SST session engages the client's emotions so that they can feel and process at the same time. Too much emotion and they stop thinking. Too little emotion and both therapist and client will have an interesting, but unproductive, theoretical discussion.

### Don't push for impact

The more an SST therapist deliberately pushes for impact, the less likely it is to happen. This is another version of the 'more is less' principle.

### Don't copy other therapists' techniques

While there are some techniques that are often used in SST (see Dryden, 2019a), when it comes to techniques that will make an impact on a particular client, it is best not to use other therapists' techniques. On this point, 'made to measure' is better than 'off the peg'.

## *You never know what will have an impact on the client*

For me, one of the exciting things about being an SST therapist is that I never know what is going to happen. I may think that something will have an impact on a client, but it does not. Conversely, something will have an impact on a client that I could never predict. It is crucial that this not deter therapists from working with impact.

## Ways of increasing the impact of single sessions

With the above caveats in mind, here are a number of ways that SST therapists can increase the impact of their work with clients.

### *Understand the nuances of a client's emotions*

When a client feels understood by the therapist and the nuances of their emotions attended to, then they can search for a solution with an appropriate level of emotional engagement.

### *Use one's voice and gestures for emphasis*

I have seen and heard many therapy sessions carried out by therapists who talk with little expression and sit very still. While this may be appropriate in some circumstances, it will not necessarily make an impact on the client. I tend to vary my tone quite a bit doing therapy and use my hands quite a bit. In particular, I sometimes use my voice in the same way as I use a highlighter – to emphasise particular points.

### *Use the client's own words*

When clients use certain words in referring to troublesome experiences, it is crucial that the therapist uses the same words rather than synonyms or vague terms like 'it', which lessens the impact of the therapist's later interventions.

## Identify and work with the client's imagery

Working with a client's emotion-infused imagery can be particularly powerful. The key point is that the therapist needs to ask about imagery to work with it as clients do not always mention it without being asked.

## Use self-disclosure

Therapist self-disclosure can have a profound impact on one client and leave another one cold. There are two critical points for therapists to keep in mind: (i) ask the client for permission before disclosing an experience and (ii) only share experiences where struggle preceded triumph and show the pathway from the former to the latter.

## Employ visual techniques

Visual methods can be memorable and therefore impactful. For example, I was working with a client on a weight issue when she discussed being at a party and having no control over her hand, which scooped up food. I asked her to show me what her hand did, and then I did it, which she found very funny, and it was an image that she subsequently used in dealing with her food-related impulses.

## Use humour

Humour can be an effective way of increasing impact as long as the therapist has a good sense of humour and the client responds well to it. Training therapists to use their humour is possible. Training them to be humorous is probably not.

## Show relevant 'YouTube' videos

There is a YouTube video which is pertinent to the practice of SST.[1] It shows in an impactful way the importance of doing something different, a point that it is vital for many SST clients to learn as they keep doing the same old thing and keep getting the same old results.

But how best to help them grasp this point? I have found a YouTube video which gets the point across beautifully.

A father is encouraging his very young daughter to count to '5'. She says, "1,2,3,5". Naturally, the father corrects her, "No sweetie; it's 1,2,3,*4*,5", said with mild emphasis. "No daddy", replies the little girl, "it's 1,2,3,5". The father corrects her as before, and his daughter responds as before. After several rounds of this same interaction, with the father using the fingers of his hand to stress the missing '4', with verbal emphasis of the '*4*' in his '1,2,3,*4*,5', the increasingly exasperated father appeals to his authority. "Listen, sweetie; I teach this stuff every day. I'm a teacher. It's '1,2,3,*4*,5'", said with great emphasis. His daughter responds with equal emphasis, "*No!* It's 1,2,3,5". At this point the father walks away, shaking his head, admitting defeat. At this point, the mother enters the situation. "Sweetie, your father is right, It's 1,2,3,4,5". "No, mommy, it's 1,2,3,5". After a few rounds of this, the mother changes tack. "Sweetie, count to '4'". The daughter thinks for a moment and says, "1,2,3,4". At this point, one can see on the video that the daughter has just had a light bulb moment. She now sees that '4' comes before '5'.

What this delightful video shows us is how humans can perpetuate their problems by getting locked into stuck patterns. It also shows us that we can bring about change quite quickly when we do something different which breaks the impasse. I sometimes show my SST clients this video on my tablet, when it is relevant to their experience, since its impact is more significant than anything that I can say to them on the importance of doing something different when what they are doing is not working.

### Note

1    www.youtube.com/watch?v=ZtUPKekDY7M (accessed 7th November 2018).

# 26

# Negotiating a solution

## Abstract

*In this chapter, I consider a number of issues concerning negotiating a solution with a client. I first offer an SST-based definition of a solution. Then, I distinguish between a chosen solution and a potential solution before discussing what insights working alliance theory have to offer the process of negotiating a solution. I end by outlining some of the main types of solution clients can be helped to choose and implement.*

Dictionary definitions of the word 'solution' tend to refer to a problem rather than a goal. For example, the *Oxford English Dictionary* defines a 'solution' as "a means of solving a problem or dealing with a difficult situation". This causes difficulty for solution-focused SST therapists who would rather deal with 'goals' than problems. As discussed in Chapter 21, a solution stands between a problem and a goal. Notwithstanding the preferred position of solution-focused therapists, a good solution in SST does have to render what the client regarded as a problem when they decided to seek therapy 'not a problem'. It also has to be considered as helping the client either to achieve their goal, or at least to take what is for them a significant step forward.

Given this, my definition of a solution in SST is as follows:

*A solution in SST is a means by which a client renders their problem a 'non-problem' and/or deals effectively with an adversity. It also helps the client to achieve their goal or take a significant step towards achieving it.*

This definition clearly favours SST therapists who work with problems *and* goals. For those who prefer to work with goals, I would put forward the following definition:

*A solution in SST is a means by which a client achieves their goal or takes a significant step towards achieving it.*

### The chosen solution and potential solutions

A solution tends to emerge from the part of the session where the therapist and client 'do the work'.[1] Given the focused nature of that work, the solutions that are available to the client within that context (called here 'potential' solutions) tend to be more limited than they were at the outset. For example, if somebody in Spain wants to visit a town in England and only has a day to do it, then they have a great many to choose from before they commit themself to fly into a particular airport. Once they make such a commitment, doing so limits their options.

Thus, it is significant for both client and therapist to realise that there are many potential solutions that could be chosen, and this becomes relevant if the work that the therapy dyad is doing is not progressing very well. When this happens, the therapist could say something like, "It seems to me that what we are discussing here is not quite hitting the 'spot' concerning what you want to achieve. What do you think?" If the client agrees, then they can change tack, a decision that will probably result in a different range of potential solutions being considered. When the client selects a solution, it is known as a 'chosen' solution.

### The importance of negotiating a solution

Whenever possible, the therapist and the client should negotiate a solution even if it is suggested by the therapist. Thus, family-oriented SST can involve one or two therapists working in the same room as the family with the session being observed by a team of therapists. At some point in the session, usually towards the end, a break is initiated by the therapist(s) to consult with the observing team out of the therapy room and from the resultant discussion an intervention is planned that generally involves a potential solution. However compelling this suggested solution might be, it still needs to be considered by the family, and it is possible that one or more family members may have difficulties with the solution. When this happens, the therapist(s) and family members discuss the matter until a solution that is acceptable to the family has been selected. Here, a negotiation has led to a chosen solution.

There are times, of course, when a therapy suggestion just hits the spot and this becomes the client's solution. From a working alliance perspective, the therapist and client are deemed to have agreed on the solution without any negotiation being necessary.

## Working alliance perspectives on solutions

The concept of the working alliance can inform the SST therapist as they work with a client to select a solution. Thus, a good SST therapist helps their client to select a solution that:

- will help them to achieve their goal
- they have the skills and capability to execute
- they have the confidence to execute
- has the therapeutic potency to enable the client to achieve their goal
- does not unwittingly serve to perpetuate their problem.

## Types of solutions in SST

There are several types of solutions that the client can implement in SST. The selected solution should best meet the client's current situation.

## Environmental solutions

An environmental solution involves the client changing or leaving an adverse situation which is unlikely to change.

## Behavioural solutions

A behavioural solution involves the client changing their behaviour to solve their problem.

## Cognitive solutions

A cognitive solution involves the client changing some aspect of their thinking about salient aspects of the problem. There are a number of different types of cognitive solution.

**Attitudinal change solutions.** An attitudinal change solution involves the client adopting a different evaluative stance towards the adversity.

**Inference change solutions.** An inference change solution involves the client changing a distorted inference that they have made about an adversity in the problematic situation.

**Reframe solutions.** A reframe solution involves the therapist helping the client put their problem in a new frame so that it is no longer a problem for them.

It is important to note that the above solutions can occur singly or in combination.

## Note

1    As discussed in Chapter 23, this phrase is deliberately left vague so that SST therapists can practise in ways that they find effective. Remember, in SST there is no one way of 'doing the work'.

# 27

# Practising the solution in the session

### Abstract

*In this chapter, I discuss the importance of the client practising their solution in the session (PSS). I discuss the reasons for doing so and the forms that such practice may take. I end with a caveat – while PSS is generally a good idea, there may be times where it is better for the client not to rehearse the solution.*

Once the client has selected a solution, and it has met the criteria of i) potentially dealing with the problem and/or ii) potentially achieving the goal or taking a significant step towards it, then ideally the next stage in the SST process is for the client to practise the solution in the session (PSS).

## Why PSS?

In my view, PSS helps the client answer one or more of the following questions.

### Does the solution feel right?

PSS helps the client to get a better 'feel' of the solution. The selected solution may be the best solution for the client on paper, but unless the client takes it out for a 'test run', they will not know, for certain, if it feels right enough for them to implement it in real life.

## Can the client make the solution work?

PSS helps the client to answer two questions: i) 'Can I do it?' and ii) 'Will it work?' Put more technically, such practice serves to help the client increase their efficacy expectations and outcome expectations, two cornerstones of self-efficacy theory originated by Bandura (1977).

## Does anything about the solution need to be changed?

PSS helps the person determine whether or not anything about the solution needs to be modified. Hopefully, at this stage, this will involve the client in 'fine-tuning' the solution rather than making a radical overhaul.

## Does PSS reveal any doubts, reservations and objections to the solution?

Getting the experience of implementing the solution, albeit within the context of the therapy session, sometimes reveals to the client that they have a doubt, reservation or objection (DRO) to some aspect of the solution and its implementation. PSS gives the therapist and client an opportunity to identify and address any such DROs.

Given that the results of PSS need to be processed and discussed, the therapist needs to ensure that they structure the session in such a way that time is given to such processing and discussion.

While PSS helps the client to answer one or more of the above questions, perhaps its primary purpose is to give the client a success experience so that they can take the chosen solution home with them with optimism.

### Forms of PSS

While I will briefly list the main ways in which PSS can be carried out, I do wish to stress that this is an opportunity for both therapist and client to demonstrate their creativity in devising a way of implementing PSS. All relevant points discussed in the session and client variables identified in the pre-session contact (or in the session if no such contact was made) are available to be incorporated into a PSS task.

## Behavioural practice of a behavioural solution

Behavioural practice allows the client to practise a behavioural solution. For example, a client may have chosen assertion as their solution. Here the therapist might role play the other person after being briefed by the client to put themself into the role of the other.

## Behavioural practice of a cognitive solution

Here, the client's actions help them to gain experience of their cognitive solution. An example of the latter is to be found in the work of Reinecke et al. (2013). In their single-session treatment of panic, they gave clients a cognitive rationale of panic. This states that panic stems from a catastrophic misinterpretation of anxiety, which is maintained by the use of a range of safety-seeking manoeuvres and that 'terrible' things will rarely happen to a person if they allow themself to be anxious without using these safety-seeking manoeuvres. To practise this cognitive solution, 'I can allow myself to experience anxiety without using any safety-seeking manoeuvres', clients were given an immediate opportunity to rehearse this by practising it in a locked room. Such rehearsal proved to be a vital ingredient of the effectiveness of the single session.

## Cognitive-behavioural practice of a cognitive solution

In CBT, the view is that the best way of changing an attitude is to think and act in ways that are consistent with the desired attitude. In PSS this is implemented by the client holding in mind the desired attitude while engaging in relevant behavioural practice.

## Mental rehearsal

Mental rehearsal involves the client picturing themself implementing the solution in their mind's eye. It is often referred to as imagery work. Here, the client can mentally rehearse any of the solutions mentioned above. They can do this to prepare themself to implement the solution in everyday life.

## Chairwork

Scott Kellogg (2007: 8) says that:

> ...chairwork is a psychotherapeutic technique that typically involves the use of two chairs that face one another. The patient sits in one chair and has a dialogue with an imagined family member or other person sitting in the opposite chair; alternatively, the patient moves back and forth between the two chairs and speaks from different aspects of him- or herself.

There are four ways in which chairwork can be used in PSS (see Dryden, 2019a, Kellogg, 2015):

- a dialogue with another person
- a dialogue between different parts of 'self'
- a dialogue to correct a problem within 'self' (e.g. a problematic attitude)
- role-playing.

Some solutions may not lend themselves to be practised in the session. For example, if the therapist has helped the client by encouraging them to reframe some aspect of their experience which led to the problem in the first place, then this may be difficult to be rehearsed in the session. Even if it could be practised then doing so may interfere with the impact of the reframe. It is important to remember that while it is generally a good thing for the client to practise their solution in the session, this is not universally the case.

Once the client has had an opportunity to practise their chosen solution in the session and has processed and discussed their experience with the therapist, then both are ready to bring the session to an end. This is the subject of the next chapter.

# 28

## Bringing the session to a suitable end

### Abstract

*In this chapter, I discuss five issues concerning the ending of the single session: i) helping the client to plan to implement the solution; ii) doing lapse response and relapse prevention work; iii) summarising; iv) agreeing on plans for future help and for follow-up; and v) tying up any loose ends.*

*When the client has had an opportunity to practise their chosen solution in the session, then this usually marks the ending phase of the session.*

### Helping the client to plan to implement the solution

When the client has finished practising the solution, and it has gone well, the therapist and client have a natural opportunity to discuss the client's plan to implement their solution when they need to in their everyday life. When discussing this, the client should be discouraged from adopting a waiting role concerning the adversity to which the client typically responds with their problematic response. Instead, they might be encouraged to seek out the adversity in order to implement the solution. For example, if the person has a problem with talking to people, rather than wait for someone to talk to them, they can practise their solution by initiating talking to a person.

In ongoing therapy, the therapist negotiates a specific 'home-work' task with a client and then reviews it at the following session. This does not happen in SST. Instead, the therapist helps the client to develop a *general* plan to implement the solution and encourages them to find specific ways of implementing this plan going forward.

## Doing lapse response and relapse prevention work

It is possible to distinguish between a lapse (a brief and minor return to a problem state) and a relapse (a 'back to square one' and more enduring return to a problem state). Relapse tends to occur when a client has not dealt adequately with lapses. Consequently, during the ending process, the therapist needs to help the person recognise the human tendency to lapse and to respond to a lapse as soon as it happens. If not, they increase the chances of a relapse happening. Or as I say, "To lapse is human, to relapse, supine". On this topic, Hoyt & Rosenbaum (2018: 320) suggest that the therapist ask the client a question such as:

- "Problems come and go. What would be a signal that the problems you were having were returning? How can you respond if you see that happening?"

Other questions might involve the client utilising strengths and resources, such as:

- "Which of your nominated strengths can you call on if you notice yourself slipping back into your problem?"
- "If you notice that you have lapsed, who might support you in dealing with it?"

I think that it is vital that the client should be told that if they do relapse, they should contact the therapist or agency for more help.

## Summarising

At some point during the ending phase of SST, it is useful for the client or the therapist to summarise the session and what the client is going to take away with them. My preference is for the client to summarise and I will prompt or add to the summary, if necessary. However, I will summarise if the situation warrants me to do so. Flexibility is, once again, important in SST. I think a good summary should contain (Dryden, 2019a):

- The client's problem and/or goal.
- The work done on the problem and/or towards the goal.
- What the client learned during this work.
- The solution the client selected and the strengths and resources they can draw on to deal with its implementation and any lapses experienced.

Some therapists encourage their clients to take away a written summary of what happened in the session, which features, in particular, what they learned and the chosen solution. Who writes the summary should be discussed by the therapy dyad. My preference is for the client to write the summary as doing so will be in their words and will maintain their active contribution to the process.

## Reminding the client about the agreed plans for future help and for follow-up

During the contracting phase (see Chapter 19), the therapist should have made clear to the client what the availability of future help will be, the nature of that help and how the client can access such help, if necessary. The therapist should reiterate these points at the end of the process.

Also, the therapist and client should agree on whether a follow-up session should be held, and if so, what the arrangements for that follow-up session should be. This will probably not apply to walk-in SST.

## Tying up any loose ends

When the session ends, it is essential that the client leaves with a sense of completeness and optimism about the process. If the client has any questions, then they should be encouraged to ask them. Also, if they have some doubts, reservations or objections (DROs) to any aspect of the process, they should be able to express them so that the therapist can respond. For example, the SST therapist could ask something like: "If when you get home, you realise that you wished you could have asked me something or told me something, what might that be?" or "Do you have any reservations about the work we did today that you would like to discuss with me before we finish today?" If a client goes away with an unasked and thus unanswered question or a reservation that has not been expressed and thus not dealt with, then they may not get as much from the process as they otherwise could.

# 29

## Encouraging client reflection, digestion, action and decision

### Abstract

*In this chapter, I discuss the importance of encouraging the client to use the time after the session to reflect on what they learned from it, to digest this learning and to experiment with ways of implementing this learning in several different ways. After a reasonable amount of time, they can decide whether or not they need further help. This is a feature of 'One-At-A-Time' (OAAT) Therapy. I also discuss a specific way of facilitating this 'reflection–digestion–action' process, which is a feature of 'Single-Session Integrated Cognitive Behaviour Therapy' (CBT), which I use in my private practice with clients who want to have a single session with me (Dryden, 2017).*

One of the ways of conceptualising SST is known as 'One-At-A-Time' Therapy (Hoyt, 2011), which I discussed briefly in Chapter 1. In this way of working, the client is informed at the outset that the therapist will work hard with them to address the issue for which they have sought help and that they may have further sessions which they can only book one at a time, as made clear in the name given to this version of SST. This happens as a matter of course in some walk-in clinics where a client can have a session and then 'walk back in' later. It is also a way of offering services in student counselling services so that help is accessed at the point of need. In doing so, this prevents the build-up of ever-increasing waiting lists where session-limited contracts are offered (e.g. everyone is offered six sessions) – see Chapter 4.

The advantage of OAAT Therapy is that the client knows that although they cannot book a series of sessions, they can have further sessions at times determined by them. Knowing that they can book another session, for example, is often a comfort to them and often means that the session is not used or is booked later than it would be in a 'session-series' booking approach.

## Reflection, digestion, action and decision

In 1990, BBC television launched a TV programme called *Masterchef* hosted by Lloyd Grossman where, each programme, three contestants cooked for a panel of three judges, hosted by Grossman. Before announcing the winner, Grossman would say, "We have deliberated, cogitated and digested and come to our conclusion", which became his catchphrase. What OAAT therapists should aim for, in my view is to help the client undergo a process at the end of which they can say the following: "I have reflected, digested and acted and have come to the conclusion that, at the moment, I don't need further help" or "I have reflected, digested and acted and have come to the conclusion that, at the moment, I am going to book another session".

### Reflection and digestion

In this complex, fast-paced world with easy access to smart phones and tablets, people often have to be encouraged to stop and reflect on their experiences before making informed decisions. In OAAT, once the session is over, it is vital that clients really reflect on and digest what they learned from the single session. This may be done privately or with trusted, supportive others. It may involve thinking about how they could apply their chosen solution to other situations or how they could experiment with other related solutions.

## Action

The OAAT therapist also needs to encourage their client to take action and implement their solution to the problem discussed in the session and, if necessary, to other problems. The therapist can also suggest that the client experiment with other related solutions that they may have thought about while in the reflection and digestion stage.

## Letting time pass

After an active period of reflection, digestion and action, the client can then be advised to let things settle down and let time pass to see how they feel about whether or not they need more help.

## Decision

In my view, the value of OAAT Therapy lies in the fact that the client knows that they can come back for another session if they need to, Knowing this means that they may not take up this offer, particularly if the client is doing well. If not, they can choose to come back at a time convenient to them.

## The use of the digital voice recording and transcript in SSI-CBT: Aids to reflection and digestion (Dryden, 2017)

In my private practice, I offer a single-session service which has three points of contact: i) a pre-session telephone conversation to help the client and myself to get the most out of ii) the face-to-face session and iii) a follow-up session about three months later (Dryden, 2017). As part of this 'package', I offer the client the chance to have a digital voice recording (DVR) of the face-to-face session and a written transcript of the session.

I do this to help the client review what we discussed in the session and to reflect on and digest what they learned from the experience. It also happens that when a client reviews the recording and transcript, they focus on an aspect of the session that they missed during the session itself which has significance for them. Clients, in particular, mention that they are pleased to have access to a summary of the session, whether they provided the summary or I did. Some make a copy of it and carry it around with them to review when necessary.

Some clients are pleased to have both the recording and the transcript, while others value one over the other. For example, some clients who do not like listening to their own voice prefer the transcript, while others who like listening to things 'on the go' on their smartphones favour the DVR. Given this, I provide clients with *both* the recording *and* the transcript (Dryden, 2017).

# 30

# Following-through and following-up

## Abstract

*In this final chapter, I consider issues concerning following-through and following-up. Following-through concerns what happens when a client decides to return and following-up concerns what happens when a client does not return, and the therapist wants to find out how they are doing and what their experience of SST was. As an example of the latter, I discuss how I follow-up with SST clients in my practice.*

As stressed in Chapter 28, after a person leaves the session that may turn out to be the only session they need (or not), they should have a clear idea of whether or not they can return if they need further help and how they can access that help.

## Following-through

Following-through occurs when the client returns for more help. When a client requests another session (as in OAAT Therapy), then the therapist should aim to see them very quickly to preserve the 'help at the point of need' principle that underpins SST (see Chapter 4). When the client is seen, then the therapist should ensure that there is continuity between the first OAAT session and the second. When the returning client is struggling with the problem for which they first sought help, then the therapist should find out what their experiences were of implementing the solution that the client chose. In particular, what was helpful when they did so and what did not help. Also, the therapist should find out which internal strengths and external resources the client made use of in implementing the solution and which could have been drawn upon, but were not.

The therapist is advised to discover a) whether the client needs help to retain the original solution and change some aspects of it and perhaps use internal strengths and external resources that they could have used but did not do so or b) whether they need to select and be helped to implement a different solution. If the former is the case then after the modifications have been decided upon, the client should be invited to practise it in the session, as outlined in Chapter 27. If the latter is the case, then the session will resemble the first session. Indeed, in such circumstances, it may be useful for the therapist to start from scratch unless it is clear why the solution did not work, in which case the new session can be built on such understanding. When a new solution has been chosen by the client, once again they should be invited to practise it in the session. Then, as before, the client goes away, reflects, digests, acts and lets time pass and hopefully the new solution will have yielded a better outcome. If not, the client returns for another session.

## Following-up

Following-up occurs when the client has not requested more help after the single session. The follow-up session occurs at a time agreed by the therapist and client and typically takes place about three months after the single session. There are a few people in the single-session community who think that a follow-up session is not a part of SST, which they define as one session and one session only. Most people, however, consider that a follow-up session is an integral part of SST.

### Why follow-up?

A follow-up session provides information on outcome, the client's view of the session and if relevant, the client' view of the service in which SST took place.

## *My approach to follow-up*

As an example of follow-up in SST, let me outline my approach to this issue (Dryden, 2017). At the end of the face-to-face session, I make a specific arrangement for a follow-up phone call which lasts between 20 and 30 minutes. I suggest that this session takes place three months after the face-to-face session to enable any changes the client has made to mature and be incorporated into their life. As with the pre-session contact, I stress that it is crucial for the session to be scheduled at a time and place where the client can talk free from distraction and interruption. I want the client to give me their full attention. Here is the framework I use in the follow-up session.

*Outcome.* I first inquire about matters to do with the outcome of the session. I begin by stating the reason why the client came for help originally.

- Has the issue changed (for better or worse or has there been no change)?
- What brought about the change or what made the problem stay the same?
- Have others noticed any change? If so, what have they noticed?
- Have other areas of your life changed for better or worse?

*The session.* I then ask about the client's experience of the session itself.

- What do you recall from the therapy session you had?
- What was particularly helpful or unhelpful?
- What use did you make of the session recording and transcript?
- How satisfied are you with the therapy that you received?
- Did you find the single session to be sufficient? If not, would you wish to resume therapy? If so, would you like to see another therapist?
- If you had any recommendations for improvement in the service that you received, what would they be?

*Other.*

- Is there anything else I have not specifically asked you that you would like me to know?

This brings us to the end of this book. I hope that you have found it valuable. I would welcome any feedback that you have for me. Please send an email to windy@windydryden.com.

# References

Appelbaum, S.A. (1975). Parkinson's Law in psychotherapy. *International Journal of Psychoanalytic Psychotherapy, 4*, 426–436.

Bandura, A. (1977). Self-efficacy: Toward a unifying theory of behavioral change. *Psychological Review, 84*, 191–215.

Battino, R. (2014). Expectation: The essence of very brief therapy. In M.F. Hoyt & M. Talmon (Eds.), *Capturing the Moment: Single Session Therapy and Walk-In Services* (pp. 393–406). Bethel, CT: Crown House Publishing.

Bloom, B.L. (1981). Focused single-session therapy: Initial development and evaluation. In S. Budman (Ed.), *Forms of Brief Therapy* (pp. 167–216). New York: Guilford Press.

Bloom, B.L. (1992). *Planned Short-Term Psychotherapy: A Clinical Handbook*. Boston, MA: Allyn and Bacon.

Bordin, E.S. (1979). The generalizability of the psychoanalytic concept of the working alliance. *Psychotherapy: Theory, Research and Practice, 16*, 252–260.

Boscolo, L., Cecchin, G., Hoffman, L., & Penn, P. (1987). *Milan Systemic Family Therapy*. New York: Basic Books.

Constantino, M.J., Ametrano, R.M., & Greenberg, R.P. (2012). Clinician interventions and participant characteristics that foster adaptive patient expectations for psychotherapy and psychotherapeutic change. *Psychotherapy, 49*, 557–569.

Constantino, M.J., Glass, C.R., Arnkoff, D.B., Ametrano, R.M., & Smith, J.Z. (2011). Expectations. In J.C. Norcross (Ed.), *Psychotherapy*

*Relationships that Work: Evidence-Based Responsiveness* (2nd ed.; pp. 354–376). New York: Oxford University Press.

Cummings, N.A. (1990). Brief intermittent psychotherapy through the life cycle. In J.K. Zeig & S.G. Gilligan (Eds.), *Brief Therapy: Myths, Methods and Metaphors* (pp. 169–194). New York: Brunner/Mazel.

Davis III, T.E., Ollendick, T.H., & Öst, L-G. (Eds.). (2012). *Intensive One-Session Treatment of Specific Phobias*. New York: Springer.

De Shazer, S. (1982). *Patterns of Brief Family Therapy*. New York: Guilford Press.

Dryden, W. (2006). *Counselling in a Nutshell*. London: Sage.

Dryden, W. (2011). *Counselling in a Nutshell* (2nd ed.). London: Sage.

Dryden, W. (2016). *When Time Is At a Premium: Cognitive-Behavioural Approaches to Single-Session Therapy and Very Brief Coaching*. London: Rationality Publications.

Dryden, W. (2017). *Single-Session Integrated CBT (SSI-CBT): Distinctive Features*. Abingdon, Oxon: Routledge.

Dryden, W. (2018a). *Very Brief Therapeutic Conversations*. Abingdon, Oxon: Routledge.

Dryden, W. (2018b). From problems to goals. Identifying 'good' goals in counselling and psychotherapy. In M. Cooper & D. Law (Eds.), *Working with Goals in Counselling and Psychotherapy* (pp.139–159). Oxford: Oxford University Press.

Dryden, W. (2019a). *Single-Session Therapy: 100 Key Points and Techniques*. Abingdon, Oxon: Routledge.

Dryden, W. (2019b). *The Relevance of Rational Emotive Behaviour Therapy for Modern CBT and Psychotherapy*. Abingdon, Oxon: Routledge.

Ellis, A., & Joffe, D. (2002). A study of volunteer clients who experienced live sessions of rational emotive behavior therapy in front of a public audience. *Journal of Rational-Emotive & Cognitive-Behavior Therapy, 20*, 151–158.

Findlay, R. (2007). A mandate for honesty, Jeff Young's No Bullshit Therapy: An interview. *Australian and New Zealand Journal of Family Therapy, 28*(3), 165–170.

Freud, S., & Breuer, J. (1895). *Studien Über Hysterie*. Leipzig and Vienna: Deuticke.

Garfield, S.L. (1995). *Psychotherapy: An Eclectic-Integrative Approach* (2nd ed.). New York: John Wiley & Sons.

Gonzalez, M.T., Estrada, B., & O'Hanlon, B. (2011). Possibilities and solutions: The differences that make a difference. *International Journal of Hispanic Psychology*, *3*(2), 185–200.

Goulding, M.M., & Goulding, R.L. (1979). *Changing Lives through Redecision Therapy*. New York: Grove Press.

Haley, J. (1989). *The First Therapy Session: How to Interview Clients and Identify Problems Successfully* (audiotape). San Francisco: Jossey-Bass.

Hayes, A.M., Laurenceau, J-P., Feldman, G., Strauss, J.L., & Cardaciotto, L. (2007). Change is not always linear: The study of nonlinear and discontinuous patterns of change in psychotherapy. *Clinical Psychology Review*, *27*, 715–723.

Hoyt, M.F. (1990). On time in brief therapy. In R.A. Wells & V.J. Gianetti (Eds.), *Handbook of the Brief Psychotherapies* (pp. 115–143). New York: Plenum.

Hoyt, M.F. (2000). *Some Stories Are Better than Others: Doing What Works in Brief Therapy and Managed Care*. Philadelphia: Brunner/Mazel.

Hoyt, M.F. (2011). Foreword. In A. Slive & M. Bobele (Eds.), *When One Hour Is All You Have: Effective Therapy for Walk-in Clients* (pp. xix–xv). Phoenix, AZ: Zeig, Tucker, & Theisen.

Hoyt, M.F. (2018). Single-session therapy: Stories, structures, themes, cautions, and prospects. In M.F. Hoyt, M. Bobele, A. Slive, J. Young, & M. Talmon (Eds.), *Single-Session Therapy by Walk-In or Appointment: Administrative, Clinical, and Supervisory Aspects of One-at-a-Time Services* (pp. 155–174). New York: Routledge.

Hoyt, M.F., & Rosenbaum, R. (2018). Some ways to end an SST. In M.F. Hoyt, M. Bobele, A. Slive, J. Young, & M. Talmon (Eds.), *Single-Session Therapy by Walk-In or Appointment: Administrative, Clinical, and Supervisory Aspects of One-at-a-Time Services* (pp. 318–323). New York: Routledge.

Hoyt, M.F., & Talmon, M.F. (2014a). What the literature says: An annotated bibliography. In M.F. Hoyt & M. Talmon (Eds.), *Capturing the Moment: Single Session Therapy and Walk-In Services* (pp. 487–516). Bethel, CT: Crown House Publishing.

Hoyt, M.F., & Talmon, M.F. (Eds.). (2014b). *Capturing the Moment: Single Session Therapy and Walk-In Services*. Bethel, CT: Crown House Publishing.

Hoyt, M.F., Bobele, M., Slive, A., Young, J., & Talmon, M. (2018a). Single-session/one-at-a-time walk-in therapy. In M.F. Hoyt, M. Bobele, A. Slive, J. Young, & M. Talmon (Eds.), *Single-Session Therapy by Walk-In or Appointment: Administrative, Clinical, and Supervisory Aspects of One-at-a-Time Services* (pp. 3–24). New York: Routledge.

Hoyt, M.F., Bobele, M., Slive, A., Young, J., & Talmon, M. (Eds.). (2018b). *Single-Session Therapy by Walk-In or Appointment: Administrative, Clinical, and Supervisory Aspects of One-at-a-Time Services*. New York: Routledge.

Iveson, C., George, E., & Ratner, H. (2014). Love is all around: A single session solution-focused therapy. In M. F. Hoyt & M. Talmon (Eds.), *Capturing the Moment: Single Session Therapy and Walk-In Services* (pp. 325–348). Bethel, CT: Crown House Publishing.

Jacobson, N.S., Follette, W.C., & Revenstorf, D. (1984). Psychotherapy outcome research: Methods for reporting variability and evaluating clinical significance. *Behavior Therapy*, *15*, 336–352.

Kellogg, S. (2015). *Transformational Chairwork: Using Psychotherapeutic Dialogues in Clinical Practice*. Lanham, MD: Rowman & Littlefield.

Kellogg, S.H. (2007). Transformational chairwork: Five ways of using therapeutic dialogues. *NYSPA Notebook*, *19*(4), 8–9.

Kuehn, J.L. (1965). Encounter at Leyden: Gustav Mahler consults Sigmund Freud. *Psychoanalytic Review*, *52*, 345–364.

Lambert, M.J. (2013). The efficacy and effectiveness of psychotherapy. In M.J. Lambert (Ed.), *Bergin and Garfield's Handbook of Psychotherapy and Behavior Change* (6th ed.; pp. 169–218). New York: Wiley.

Lonergan. J. (2012, Autumn). 'I alone must do it, but I cannot do it alone'. *Inside Out*, Issue 68. [http://iahip.org/inside-out/issue-68-autumn-2012/i-alone-must-do-it-but-i-cannot-do-it-alone-a-talk-by-john-lonergan-a-decade-on-10th-anniversary-celebration-of-inside-out] (accessed 7th November 2018).

McElheran, N., Stewart, J., Soenen, D., Newman, J., & MacLaurin. B. (2014). Walk-in single session therapy at the Eastside Family Centre. In M.F. Hoyt & M. Talmon (Eds.), *Capturing the Moment:Single Session Therapy and Walk-In Services* (pp. 177–195). Bethel, CT: Crown House Publishing.

Miller, W.R., & C' de Baca, J. (2001). *Quantum Change: When Epiphanies and Sudden Insights Transform Ordinary Lives*. New York: Guilford.

O'Hanlon, W.H., & Hexum, A.L. (1990). *An Uncommon Casebook: The Complete Clinical Work of Milton H. Erickson M.D.* New York: Norton.

Paul, K.E., & van Ommeren, P. (2013). A primer on single session therapy and its potential application in humanitarian situations. *Intervention*, *11*(1), 8–23.

Pitman, J. (2017). *The Invisible Man: The Story of Rod Temperton, the 'Thriller' Songwriter.* Stroud, Gloucestershire: The History Press.

Prochaska, J.O., Norcross, J.C., & DiClemente, C.C. (2006). *Changing for Good: A Revolutionary Six-Stage Program for Overcoming Bad Habits and Moving Your Life Positively Forward*. New York: Harper Collins.

Ratner, H., George, E., & Iveson, C. (2012). *Solution Focused Brief Therapy: 100 Key Points and Techniques*. Hove, East Sussex: Routledge.

Reinecke, A., Waldenmaier, L., Cooper, M.J., & Harmer, C.J. (2013). Changes in automatic threat processing precede and predict clinical changes with exposure-based cognitive-behavior therapy for panic disorder. *Biological Psychiatry*, *73*, 1064–1070.

Rogers, C.R. (1957). The necessary and sufficient conditions of therapeutic personality change. *Journal of Consulting Psychology*, *21*, 95–103.

Rosenthal, R., & Jacobson, L. (1968). *Pygmalion in the Classroom: Teacher Expectation and Pupils' Intellectual Development*. New York: Holt, Rinehart & Winston.

Simon, G.E., Imel, Z.E., Ludman, E.J., & Steinfeld, B.J. (2012). Is dropout after a first psychotherapy visit always a bad outcome? *Psychiatric Services*, *63*(7), 705–707.

Talmon, M. (1990). *Single Session Therapy: Maximising the Effect of the First (and Often Only) Therapeutic Encounter.* San Francisco: Jossey-Bass.

Talmon, M. (1993). *Single Session Solutions: A Guide to Practical, Effective and Affordable Therapy*. New York: Addison-Wesley.

Talmon, M. (2018). The eternal now: On becoming and being a single-session therapist. In M.F. Hoyt, M. Bobele, A. Slive, J. Young, & M.

Talmon (Eds.), *Single-Session Therapy by Walk-In or Appointment: Administrative, Clinical, and Supervisory Aspects of One-at-a Time Services* (pp. 149–154). New York: Routledge.

Young, J. (2018). SST: The misunderstood gift that keeps on giving. In M.F. Hoyt, M. Bobele, A. Slive, J. Young, & M. Talmon (Eds.), *Single-Session Therapy by Walk-In or Appointment: Administrative, Clinical, and Supervisory Aspects of One-at-a-Time Services* (pp. 40–58). New York: Routledge.

# Index

*Note*: Page numbers in **bold** refer to tables.

ABC framework 117
active-directive tradition 33,
    116–118
adversities 41, **42**, 43, 75, 117, 140
Ametrano, R.M. 26
applicant role 87, 88–89
appointments 6, 82, 86, 96, 121
appropriate action 14
Arts University of Bournemouth
    (AUB) 16–17
as-if principle 22
attitude change 40–41, 118, 134, 138

Battino, R. 27
behavioural solutions 134, 137
behavioural tasks 100–102
behaviour change 39–41, 134
Bobele, M. 4, 30, 33, 115, 116
bonds 56–58, 65
Bordin, E.S. 59
Brief Family Therapy Center,
    Milwaukee 27
brief intermittent psychotherapy 5

Cardaciotto, L. 37
case conceptualisation 75–76

CBT (cognitive behavioural
    therapy) 76, 117, 137
chairwork 138
change 12–14, 36–37, 67–69;
    attitude 40–41, 118, 134, 138;
    behaviour 39–41, 134
*Christmas Carol, A*
    (Dickens) 39–40
client criteria 38, 44–45, **46–47**, 48
client empowerment 30–31, 70,
    82–83, 121
client history 73
client plans 141
client role 87
client strengths 22–23, 31–32, 54,
    70, 122
client summaries 83, 102–103,
    142, 146–147
client variables 114, 121–125
cognitive solutions 134, 137–138
collaborative relationship
    59, 61, 65
Constantino, M.J. 26
constructive tradition 33,
    115–116, 119
contemplator role 86–87

contracts 95, 142
Cooper, M.J. 137
core conditions 60–62
Cummings, N. 5

demonstration sessions 41, 48, **49**
de Shazer, S. 27
digital voice recordings *see* DVRs
doing tasks 100–102
drop-in services 17, 19
drop-outs 6
DROs (doubts, reservations or objections) 136, 143
Dryden, W. 23, 27–28, 41, 87–88, 95–96, 116; client summaries 142; DVRs 146–147; expectations 29; follow-ups 150–151; goals 117; interrupting 22, 112; OAAT therapy 4, 144; pre-session telephone contact 87–88, 91, 118; problem assessment 75, 117, 118; problem solving 123–124; solutions 121; SST 7, 8, 51, 75, 98; student counselling 16; VBTCs 41, 48, **49**
duration expectations 26–27
DVRs (digital voice recordings) 146–147

Ellis, A. 5
email summaries 102–103
embedded SST 45, 53, 57
emotions 41, **42**, **49**, 118–119
empathy 60
enquirer role 87, 88
environmental solutions 134
expectations 24–25, 26–29
expertise 33–34, 102, 114
external resources 32, 68, 83, 148

face-to-face meetings 3, 4, 91
Feldman, G. 37

follow-throughs 83, 148–149
follow-ups 23, 83, 142–143, 146, 149–151
future help 142–143, 146, 148–151

generalisation 116
genuineness 61
goals 28, 54–55, 59, 63, 105–106, 107–109, 117, 121
good practice guidelines 65–70, 72–77
Greenberg, R.P. 26
guiding principles 32

Harmer, C.J. 137
Harry (behavioural task example) 100–102
Hayes, A.M. 37
help-seeking roles 86–89
Hoyt, M.F. 4, 5, 9, 26–27, 30, 33, 38, 81, 84, 115, 116, 141
humour 129

imagery work 64, 129, 138
Imel, Z.E. 36
impact 126–130
inference change solutions 134
in-session practice 67, 70, 135–139, 140
internal strengths 31–32, 122, 148
interrupting 22, 111–113
interventions 83, 118

Jacobson, L. 28
Jane (social anxiety example) 123–124
Jerry (guilt example) 124–125

Kellogg, S.H. 138
knowledge 12–13

Lambert, M.J. 36
lapses 141

Laurenceau, J-P. 37
Ludman, E.J. 36

McElheran, N. 81, 84
MacLaurin, B. 81, 84
Martha (adversities example) 43
mental rehearsal 64, 129, 138

NBT (No Bullshit Therapy) 61
negotiated goals 107–109
negotiated solutions 67, 70, 83,
    105–106, 132–133, 141
Newman, J. 81, 84
NHS (National Health
    Service) 17, 19
noticing tasks 100

OAAT (one-at-a-time) therapy
    4–5, 6, 16–17, 83–84, 97,
    144–146
other people 31–32
outcome expectations 26,
    27–28

panic 137
pathways 56
Paul (fear of heights example)
    11–12, 13, 14
pluralistic tradition 33, 118–119
point of availability, help at 8, 16,
    17, **18–19**, 56
point of need, help at 8, 16, 17,
    **18–19**, 56
potential solutions 132
pre-session contact 99–100, 102;
    telephone contact 91,
    102–103, 118
pre-session questionnaire 91, **92**
problem assessment 75, 117
problematic emotions *see*
    emotions
problem-focused SST 103
problems 105–107, 121

problem solving 31, 40–41,
    54–55, 64, 70, 82–83, 123–124,
    145–146
process expectations 26
PSS (practise the solution in the
    session) 67, 70, 135–139, 141
psychological services 16–17
psychotherapy 5, 26, 28, 36–37,
    39; Parkinson's law of 27
pupil performance 28

quantum change 39
questions 77, 122

rapid change 12–14
reason, change commitment 13
REBT (Rational Emotive
    Behaviour Therapy) 5, 41, 117
reframe solutions 134, 138
Reinecke, A. 137
relapses 141
resources 23, 32, 68, 83, 148
respect 60
Rogers, C.R. 60
role expectations 26
role models 32, 114–115
Rosenbaum, R. 141
Rosenthal, R. 28

self-disclosure 129
session preparation 90–93
session recording 98, 146–147
Simon, G.E. 36
Slive, A. 4, 30, 33, 115, 116
SMART goals 108–109
Soenen, D. 81, 84
solution-focused SST 103, 121
solutions 123–124, 131–134,
    145–146; in-session practice 67,
    70, 135–139, 141; negotiated 67,
    70, 83, 105–106, 132–133, 141
SST (Single-Session Therapy)
    3–4, 5–6, 7–10, 33, 36,

51–55, 95–96, 98; good practice guidelines 65–70, 72–77; process 81–85, 141
SST clients 10, 15–16, 19–20, 23, 35–37, 41, 50, 51–52, 73–74; client criteria 38, 44–45, **46–47**, 48; SST mindset 21, 22, 24–25, 27–28
SST fusion 30, 33, 83
SST mindset 21–22, 35; SST clients 21, 22, 24–25, 27–28; SST therapists 21, 24, 25, 31
SST services 53–55
SST therapists 4, 6, 8, 9, 10, 15, 22–23, 33–34, 52–54, 69–70; client criteria 44–45; good practice guidelines 72–77; SST mindset 21, 24, 25, 29
SST traditions 114–115; active-directive tradition 33, 116–118; constructive tradition 33, 115–116, 119; pluralistic tradition 33, 118–119
Steinfeld, B.J. 36
Stewart, J. 81, 84
Strauss, J.L. 37
student counselling 16
suitability *see* client criteria

Talking Shops (drop-in service) 17–18, 19
Talmon, M.F. 4, 30, 33, 38, 100, 115, 116, 118–119

tasks 59, 63–64, 100–101
teacher expectations 28
telephone contact, pre-session 87–88, 91, 102, 118
Temperton, R. 14
therapeutic change *see* change
therapeutic focus 52–53, 66, 74, 111
therapeutic relationships 35
therapeutic services 7–10
therapist expectations 28
therapist training 36

unstuck 40

values 31
VBTCs (Very Brief Therapeutic Conversations) 41, 48, **49**
Victoria, Australia 57
views 59, 62–63
visual techniques 129

Waldenmaier, L. 137
walk-in therapy 6, 45, 81, 82, 84–85, 86, 96–97, 121, 144; pre-session questionnaire 91, **92**
working alliance 21, 24, 25, 35–36, 53, 59–64, 110, 133

Young, J. 4, 21, 22, 23, 24, 30, 33, 45, 57, 58, 61, 115, 116
YouTube videos 129–130